CALIFORNIA'S GOLDEN AGE

With Illustrations and Text
by
WILLIAM WOOLLETT, F.A.I.A.

Introduction by DAVID GEBHARD

CAPRA PRESS
SANTA BARBARA

Copyright ©1989 by the William Woollett Trust.
All rights reserved.
Printed in the United States of America.

Cover and book design by Cyndi Brooks.
Typography by Jim Cook/Santa Barbara

LIBRARY OF CONGRESS CATALGING-IN-PUBLICATION DATA
Woollett, William, 1901–
 California's golden age: as seen by William Woollett / William Woollett; introduction by David Gebhard.
  p. cm.
  ISBN 0-88496-301-2 : $12.50
  1. Woollett, William, 1901– 2. California in art.
3. Buildings in art. I. Title.
NC139.W67A4 1989
741.973—dc19   88.37649 CIP

CAPRA PRESS
Post Office Box 2068 / Santa Barbara, California 93120

CONTENTS

I. INTRODUCTION 7

II. FOREWORD 11

III. DEDICATION 13

IV. LOS ANGELES 15
   A. Introduction 17
   B. Illustrations
      1. Olvera Street overview 19
      2. Olvera Street doorway with woman 20
      3. Olvera Street window and lamp 22
      4. Olvera Street prayer shrine 23
      5. Olvera Street outdoor shop 24
      6. Pico House 25
      7. Hollywood Bowl 26
      8. Pilgrimage Play Theater 28
      9. Pilgrimage Play Theater 29
     10. Plaza Church 30
     11. Silver Lake 31
     12. La Brea Adobe 32
     13. La Brea Tar Pits 34
     14. Presbyterian Church 35
     15. L.A. River Bridge 36
     16. Old winery 37
     17. World Premier 38
     18. Cerritos Adobe 39
     19. San Pedro Harbor 40
     20. Griffith Observatory 41
     21. Pasadena Bridge (distant view) 42
     22. Pasadena Bridge (close-up) 43
     23. Bullocks Department Store 44

V. SAN DIEGO 47
   A. Introduction 48
   B. Illustrations
      1. Main entrance to the Fair 49
      2. Horticultural Building 50
      3. Fiesta dancers 51

  4. Statuette 52
  5. Fair buildings 53
  6. Court of the Seasons 54

VI. CALIFORNIA MISSIONS 57
 A. Introduction 58
 B. Illustrations
  1. San Gabriel Arcangel 59
  2. San Juan Capistrano 60
  3. San Juan Capistrano 61
  4. Santa Barbara 62
  5. San Fernando Rey de España 63
  6. San Fernando Rey de España 64
  7. San Fernando Rey de España 65
  8. Santa Ínez 66

VII. CATALINA ISLAND 69
 A. Introduction 70
 B. Illustrations
  1. Wrigley Mansion 71
  2. Harbor View .72
  3. Central Square 73
  4. Harbor view .74
  5. Boats in the harbor 75
  6. Hotel St. Catherine's 76
  7. Pavilion 77
  8. Promenade and bell tower 78
  9. Pavilion 79
  10. Pavilion 80
  11. Clubhouse 81

VIII. HOOVER DAM 83
 A. Introduction 84
 B. Illustrations
  1. Highscaler 86
  2. Nearly finished dam 89

IX. TRANSMISSION LINES 91
 A. Introduction 92

    B. Illustrations
       1. Surveying 94
       2. Road Scraper .95
       3. Desert crew 96
       4. Concrete down chute 97
       5. On-site 98
       6. Steel tower legs 99
       7. Early morning light 100
       8. Tool shed 101
       9. Half-built tower 102
     10. Nearly completed tower 103
     11. Completed towers 104
     12. Factory 105
     13. Tractor and ground wire 106

X. AQUEDUCT 109
    A. Introduction 110
    B. Illustrations
       1. View through the desert 111
       2. Tunnel entrance 112

XI. ALL-AMERICAN CANAL 115
    A. Introduction 116
    B. Illustration: Digging 117

XII. SAN FRANCISCO 119
    A. Introduction 120
    B. Illustrations
       1. Golden Gate Bridge
          a. Without cables 122
          b. With cables 124
       2. Oakland-Bay Bridge
          a. View from Oakland 125
          b. Rock and gravel 126
          c. Four towers 127
          d. First tower—Yerba Buena 128
          e. First pier .129
          f. Tunnel—Yerba Buena 130
          g. Bay Bridge anchorage 131

      h. Second bridge tower 132
      i. Bridge towers 133
      j. Steel section of bridge 134
      k. Cantilevered section 135
      l. Scow and bridge support 136
3. General
      a. Overview of San Franscisco 138
      b. Chinatown 140

INTRODUCTION

DAVID GEBHARD

IN THE YEAR 1935, in the midst of the Great Depression of the 1930s, the young Los Angeles architect, William Woollett (1901-1988), exhibited two strikingly different exhibitions of his prints and drawings. At the Natural History Building of the U.S. National Museum in Washington, D.C. he presented a group of his lithographs which depicted various phases of the construction of Hoover (Boulder) Dam. A few months later, at the Architect's Building on West 5th Street in Los Angeles, a selection of his drawings and prints was exhibited under the title, "Anchors of the Past: Early California Exhibit." These two exhibitions beautifully sum up two strong and quite opposite pulls which came to characterize the decade of the thirties: Hoover Dam as a potent symbol of faith in progress and technology; and then the antithesis of this faith in the science fiction world of the future; the recurring desire to look back to the idyllic moments of the past, in this instance, California's early nineteenth-century Hispanic world.

Such pulls in opposite directions had, of course, characterized the years before 1930, but the social and economic implications of the Depression accentuated this duality of response. For those who then as well as now insist on a black-and-white world of either/or, such seemingly inimical beliefs are generally deplored. But the pull of opposites was part of the richness of response (both positive and negative) at the time, and it would certainly be difficult for us today to gain a sense of the thirties without taking it into account.

As with other architects educated in the 1920s and before, William Woollett had the advantage of an architectural education through the French-inspired Beaux Arts tradition. Through his experiences at the University of Minnesota, in attending the A.I.A. sponsored Beaux Arts Program in New York, and in his work as a draftsman in the New York offices of James Gamble Rogers and Alexander Trowbridge, Woollett not only acquired his skills in the graphic arts, but also in the characteristic belief of the American architectural profession that a successful solution to any architectural problem entailed using the past as a starting point for the present and the future.

Woollett's first drawings and prints (lithographs and etchings) outside of the direct practice of architecture were made between 1925 and 1929 when he was working in the Los Angeles office of his father, William Lee Woollett. At this time he divided his attention between depicting new contemporary buildings in Los Angeles—such as his drawings of the exterior and interiors of John and Donald Parkinson's Art Deco masterpiece, Bullock's Wilshire department store (1928)—to glances back into the past, such as his sketches of Olvera Street. Not only was his subject matter varied, but so were his aesthetic techniques. Some of these prints and drawings closely reflect the rendering style of the then-popular graphic artist, Samuel Chamberlain; others indicate a response to the more abstract tradition of the architectural renderer Hugh Ferriss and his cities of the future.

With the nationwide effect of the Depression sharply curtailing architectural practice, Woollett decided to turn his attention to a series of great engineering projects being built in California during the 1930s. His goal was to depict these projects through their various stages of construction. In this approach he was taking a direct clue from the great turn-of-the-century graphic artist, Joseph Pennell, who had illustrated the construction of the Panama Canal in a 1912 volume, *Pictures of the Panama Canal* (New York: Lippincott). Woollett's first endeavor concentrated on the construction of Hoover Dam (this was first published by Woollett in 1932 as *Hoover Dam Project, A Complete Story of its Construction in Pictures from Lithographs and Sketches* (Los Angeles: privately published).

Later in the decade he depicted the construction of the All-American Canal, the Transmission Line, the Los Angeles Aqueduct (from Hoover Dam), and the two great bridge projects in the San Francisco Bay Area—the Golden Gate Bridge and the Bay Bridge. But this energetic interest in present and future technology did not prevent Woollett from continually turning his attention to California's past. From these years date his series on Bertram G. Goodhue's 1915 Exposition in Balboa Park in San Diego, views of the Pasadena Bridge over the Arroyo Seco, and others.

With the resumption of building activity after World War II, Woollett returned to his architectural practice. He still found time, though, to continue to sketch and draw historic scenes and buildings throughout California. In the early 1960s he, along with Carl Dentzel, helped to draw up Los Angeles' first Historic Preservation Ordinance, and served for a number of years (1962-1972) on the commission which administered it, the Los Angeles Cultural Heritage Commission. (See his article, "Los Angeles Landmarks," published in *Historic Preservation,* July-August, 199X: pp. 160-163). When he later moved to Santa Barbara his commitment to history and preservation continued with his membership on the city's Advisory Landmark Committee (along with Pearl Chase, Lutah Maria Riggs, and others).

William Woollett's last years were taken up with preparing a volume on his experience in recording the construction of Hoover Dam (*Hoover Dam: Drawings, Etchings, Lithographs, 1931-1933,* Los Angeles: Hennessey & Ingalls, 1986). At the time of his death in late 1988, he had completed the text and the assembage of his graphic material for this present volume. Through his prints and drawings, and his writings about them, we today can discern how a sensitive architect/artist responded over a period of half a century to a series of changing visions of California's past, present, and future.

FOREWORD

MOST PEOPLE today were not alive or cannot remember California as it was in the early days of the twentieth century. With the population increasing rapidly, California faced many problems of supplying adequate water, transportation and electrical power for her people. Thus California was forced to develop many of her natural resources for the public good.

I like to think of this period as California's Golden Age. It was a period during which Californa's resources were first tested and developed.

I can remember those early days, for I was still a young man when there were no bridges across the San Francisco Bay, and everyone had to take the ferry from Oakland to San Francisco. Later I lived in Los Angeles when there was a shortage of water, before the Hoover Dam tamed the Colorado River and diverted its water supply and electrical power to southern California.

Many engineering and architectural wonders such as the San Francisco bridges and the Hoover Dam quite dramatically changed the way of life throughout the state and helped bring into use other of her natural resources, such as the rich farmland of the San Joaquin, Coachella, and Imperial valleys.

In those early days I was an architect, but when jobs were scarce, I found work as an artist, and I was especially impressed with some of these amazing monumental structures as they were being built. I wanted to make sketches of these works as they progressed in order to capture the story of their actual construction for future generations.

In addition, I was interested in drawing historic buildings that I thought were a vital part of the record of California's early cultural development.

My collection of original lithographs, sketches, and etchings dates back to 1915. Many of these have been published in various forms, including a recent book in which I wrote about the construction of the Hoover Dam (with an assist from the National Endowment for the Arts). Much of my work has been on display around the country through public exhibition, in libraries and universities, and at the National Gallery of Art in Washington, D.C. All of this work is illustrated by either lithographs, sketches, or etchings, most of which were made on the site. It is my hope this book will help the reader appreciate how the development of some of western America's natural resources was achieved.

This book is dedicated
to my four sons
WILLIAM 2nd, JAMES, JOSEPH and MORGAN
who have shared with "Dad" many
of the growing up days
of California living, with its memories,
its aspirations and defeats.
This has made the writing of this book
a joy and a pleasure.

Los Angeles

LOS ANGELES

WHEN I WAS fourteen my parents moved from San Francisco to Los Angeles. After finishing Hollywood High School I studied architecture at the University of Minnesota, following the profession of my father. I then continued study at L'École de Beaux Arts in New York and became a fourth-generation architect.

Unfortunately, when I returned to Los Angeles in 1923, there was little demand for young architects. Throughout the next decade of high unemployment in America, necessity became the mother of invention for me and a host of others.

Many professionals took menial jobs as plumbers, watchmen, factory workers, elevator operators or almost anything else which could help to feed their families. Then it was that I turned my attention to my love for drawing and hoped to make a decent living.

The first thing to do, of course, was to assemble a portfolio of my work. My father told me an artist needs to draw at least two hundred pictures in order to develop skill. Consequently, I roamed Los Angeles with a sketch pad and drew almost anything which appealed to me in order to gain proficiency and develop my portfolio.

As I began selling my work, I also learned to barter sketches for the things I needed, whether it was a plane ticket, an overcoat, a vacation or drawing materials.

Thus I began my career in Los Angeles, where I lived for sixty years, as the city grew from a half million people to more than six million. There I found employment first as an artist and eventually as an architect. In those years I came to appreciate more of California's history and natural resources. I also began to see what I might do to help preserve that legacy for the future. From the eighteenth-century mission days the city of Los Angeles had been a megalopolis of sorts. In those early years, small, almost-isolated communities grew up with such names as Hollywood, Pasadena, Beverly Hills, and Watts.

Originally, they "grew like topsy," as Mrs. A.S.C. Forbes recorded in her historical account, *The Days of the Dons*. Early settlers who had received land grants from the Spanish government often lived the lives of country gentlemen, but much of this changed as five separate wars and the period of the Gold Rush brought an influx of thousands from the eastern states and abroad.

In this century, expansion in the Los Angeles area was made possible largely because of a system of pipelines and aqueducts which brought water from the Sierra Nevadas and the Colorado River, three hundred miles away.

Those small early towns scattered in the Los Angeles area have grown to the point where their boundaries touch and most vacant lots have disappeared. Now greater Los Angeles has become the second largest city in the United States.

In order to accommodate this rapid growth, many of the old buildings were being destroyed. I was keenly aware of this because of my role as the chairman of the American Institute of Architect's Committee on Historic Preservation.

One day in the early 1960s I was walking down the street and turned the corner to see workmen demolishing one of the beautiful buildings I had recently sketched. Then and there I determined to do something about the destruction of Los Angeles' historic landmarks.

I gathered what influential support I could to help in the founding of the city's Cultural Heritage Board (1962). Then we pushed for legislation which would put teeth in preservation efforts, not only in Los Angeles, but also on the state and national level.

Whenever possible, I wanted future generations to see the original structures and not just photographs and sketches of these historic places.

OLVERA STREET OVERVIEW

Some of my earliest etchings were scenes drawn at a Los Angeles treasure spot called Olvera Street. "Little Mexico," as it is sometimes called, is full of shops with imported wares, making it a colorful Mexican enclave.

My father had been working at the Civic Center, seen in the background of the picture. He introduced me to his friend Mrs. Sterling who owned a shop above the famous La Golondrina Restaurant. She befriended me as I was making this series of etchings.

That evening, I remember being intrigued by the appearance of an old Mexican woman in a booth. Although Olvera Street was a mecca for tourists, I was drawn back time and time again because the variety and activity gave me such a fine setting to draw.

1925, etching, 7½" x 5"

19

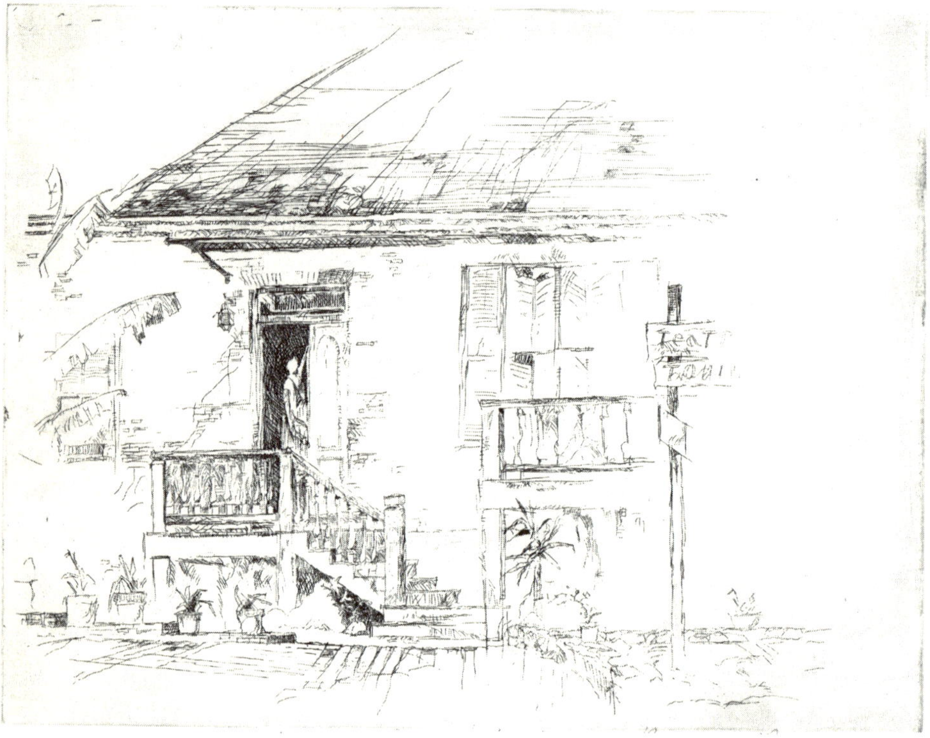

WOMAN IN DOORWAY

The driving force behind the development of Olvera Street was Mrs. Christine Sterling, a descendent of an early California family. Early Olvera Street was a muddy back alley between Main and Spring Streets when Mrs. Sterling observed the popularity of the few ethnic shops there, also noting that winter rains made shopping nearly impossible.

Envisioning the possibilities for Olvera Street's development, she enlisted the aid of Harry Chandler, owner of the Los Angeles Times, to help promote this unique gathering place. Mrs. Sterling's sister, Genevieve Rix Burrows, is pictured here in the doorway of the shop. Here also is where I met a woman who was to have a great influence on my professional life. Mrs. Armitage Forbes was committed to the preservation of California history and became my good friend and mentor. I spent many hours poring over her history books and listening to stories about early days in California.

1925, etching, 6" x 7½"

OLVERA STREET WINDOW AND LAMP

This is a typical Olvera Street shop with its South-of-the-Border flavor. This little building was used by the Yale players for years as a theater, and Olvera Street became a popular place for browsing and eating after performances.

1925, etching, 6" x 8"

OLVERA STREET PRAYER SHRINE

This little shrine provides a quiet setting not only for the devout, but also for the budding entrepreneur. A sleepy man relaxes while his shoes are being worked on by a boy.

Note the contrast of the natural gas tank partially hidden by an old brick wall in the background. The tripod standing to the left provides shade.

1925, etching, 8" x 6"

OLVERA STREET OUTDOOR SHOP

This is the entrance to the Avila Adobe where a man tends his open air shop near a large tripod-supported sunshade.

The Adobe is designated a California historic landmark. In 1846 a treaty between California and Mexico was signed here by Captain John Fremont of the U.S. Army and General Pio Pico, governor of California.

Two years later gold was discovered in Northern California, signalling the beginning of a mass migration from the East Coast. Then, on September 9, 1850, California became a state. This picture shows the Old World character of the Mexican enclave amid the Americanization of the area.

1925, etching, 6" x 8"

THE PICO HOUSE

The Pico House, near Olvera, on the corner of Sunset Boulevard and Main Street, is one of the early buildings reflecting typical Midwestern architecture. The house draws its name from a governor of California when it was under Mexican rule. General Pio Pico was the military commander in 1846 who resisted the American forces led by Captain Fremont.

The brick building trimmed with wood was the first hotel of any prominence. It adjoined the Los Angeles Plaza on the east near the entrance to the early railroad station. The small building to the south of Pico House was the only movie theater in the area for many years.

Fremont's widow, Jesse, was still alive when I made these drawings, and she owned the flags her husband had captured in his battles. She too was a close friend of Mrs. Forbes, who decided these flags should be housed in a permanent exhibit. She persuaded the city to buy the open field where Fremont and Pico had met on the Los Angeles River below Cahuenga Pass. She then convinced them to erect Campo de Cahuenga, a recreational building, to display the flags. She and I founded the Campo de Cahuenga Society, and I became its first president. Later the field itself was made into a park.

1925, charcoal, 11″ x 13½″

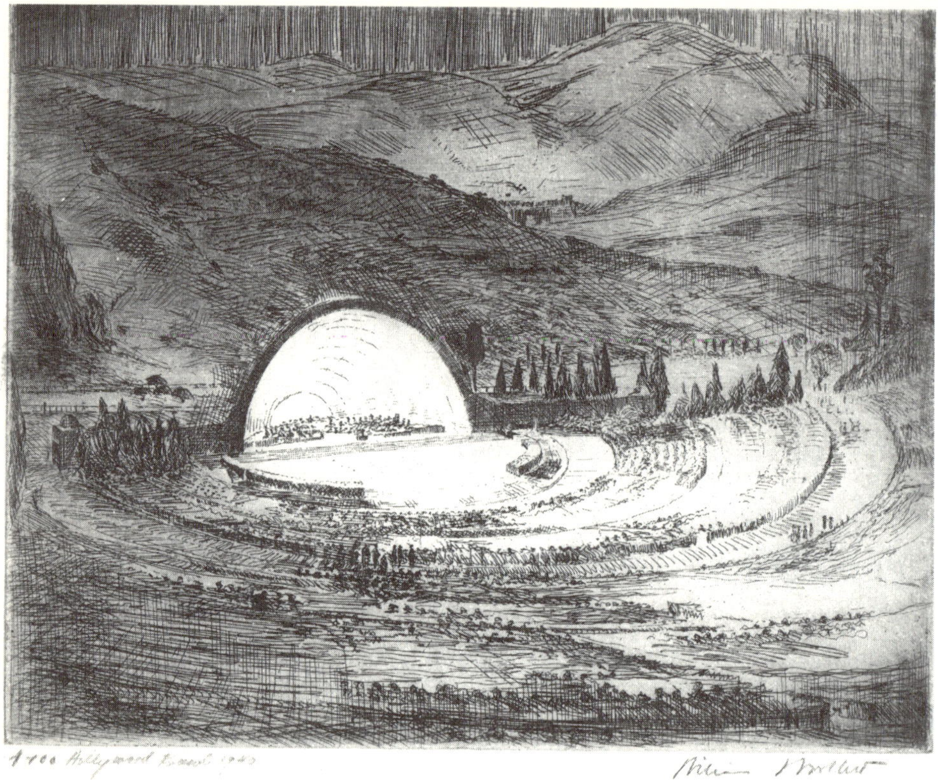

HOLLYWOOD BOWL

After the turn of the century local interest grew for an amphitheater for the performing arts. A small canyon just south of the city's entrance to the San Fernando Valley made an ideal location. Early plans for the Bowl were drawn by architect William Lee Woollett, yet the building was a truly local effort, joined by prominent citizens and leaders of the motion picture industry.

Originally, the audience sat on the hillside. Later, funds were raised to provide rough seating for more than six thousand people. Many of the early performances were held on a makeshift platform built from props supplied by some of the movie studios.

Mrs. Artie Carter, president of the Woman's Club of Hollywood, became president of the Hollywood Bowl Association. Her appointment of various committees aroused enthusiasm for the Bowl. As more funds were raised, the actual Bowl was created by excavation, and permanent benches were installed along with a grander stage enclosed by a protective shell.

1940, etching, 7" x 9"

PILGRIMAGE PLAY THEATER

The Pilgrimage Play Theater, near the Hollywood Bowl, was built in 1925 after a strong community effort led by Mrs. Christine Witherel Stevenson. Much of the cost of funding came from local citizens, although the theater was actually built and paid for by Los Angeles County. Volunteer help from well-known directors and stage designers provided opportunities to many young Hollywood stars who made their debuts on this stage. The theater was remodeled in the 1970s and renamed the John Anson Ford Theater.

1925, etching, 6" x 8"

PILGRAIMAGE PLAY THEATER

Here we see the construction of the back wall of the Pilgrimage Play Theater building, whose lights could be seen at night from the Hollwyood Bowl across nearby Highland Avenue.

The theater was designed by my father, William Lee Woollett, pioneer Los Angeles architect.

It could accommodate about 900 people and became a very popular place, with a full house every night during the summer season.

A stage was located at the mouth of a small ravine that extended back into the hill about a hundred feet and served as a dressing area.

The only production there was *The Christ Play*, a two-hour review of the events of Jesus' life, using much of the Biblical narrative. The play could well have developed into another *Oberamergau*.

1925, etching, 6" x 8"

PLAZA CHURCH

The Plaza Church was part of the early development of Los Angeles and contains many relics of the city's history. It is located on the north end of the Civic Center, across from Pico House. The churchyard behind the large magnolia tree contains many Indian graves and those of early Los Angeles residents. Dating from the middle of the nineteenth century, the church was built of adobe blocks and has three old bells from Mexico.

c. 1928, etching, 8" x 6"

SILVER LAKE

Among the hills of Los Angeles lies a beautiful valley which brings back many lovely memories. The area was appropriately called Edendale.

Silver Lake was located in this valley, and I remember many picnics and boat outings there. We liked to watch the clouds reflected in the lake, creating a shimmering picture on the wind-tossed ripples.

Many fine homes were built in the surrounding hills, and the area was serviced by a small trolley line which carried passengers into Los Angeles proper. As more and more people found Edendale, there was a greater demand for roads to connect this then-remote area to the city. Before long, these thoroughfares made the trolley line obsolete.

Many of the charming old homes still cling to the steep-sided hills, although this special place is no longer isolated.

c. 1926, etching, 7½" x 9"

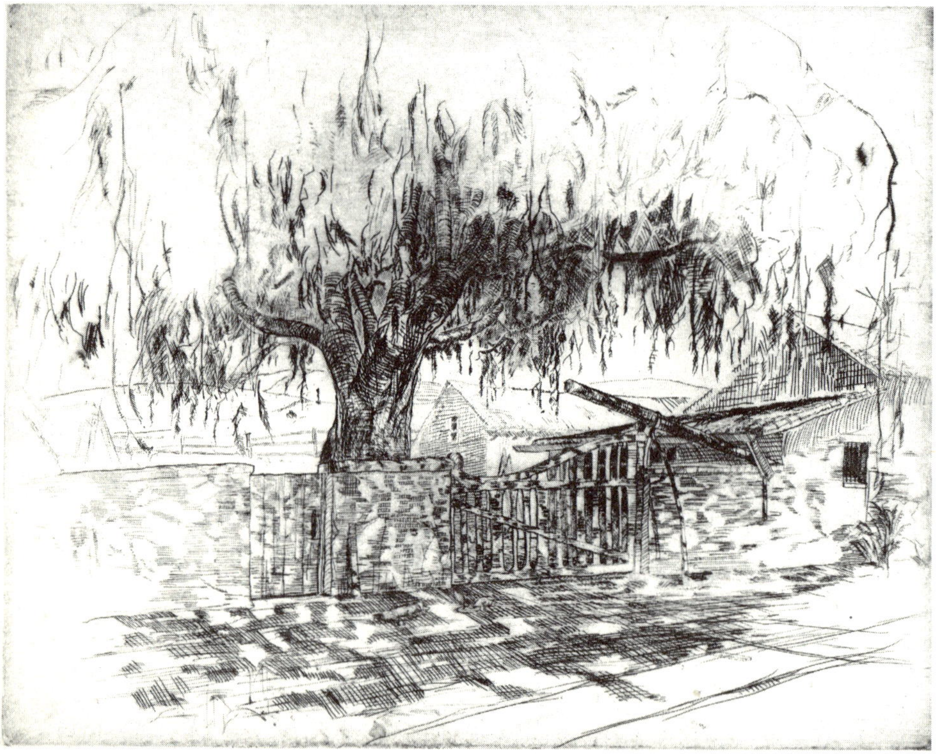

LA BREA ADOBE

In Los Angeles, the La Brea Adobe was the oldest building of its kind still standing while much of the city grew up around it. La Brea had the look of an old farmhouse and was made of adobe blocks by early Indians who had lived in the area.

A beautiful large pepper tree shaded much of the back yard, which was surrounded by adobe walls. A log was positioned to control the gate, forcing it to close once it was opened.

In the early part of the century, La Brea Adobe was owned by oilman Earl Gilmore, and thus it came to be known as the Gilmore Adobe. During the years he lived there, major oil deposits were discovered in the area. He wanted to remain in his home, but the land become extremely valuable, so he sold it, and the house was demolished. Developers built tract homes there which were later moved to make way for drilling.

c. 1926, etching, 7" x 9"

LA BREA TAR PITS

During the early days, when oil was discovered in Los Angeles, rigs were erected in the fields near what is now the intersection of La Brea Avenue and Wilshire Boulevard.

Drilling produced much of the tar for the roofing of houses and the surfacing of streets in the Los Angeles area. Work at the La Brea Tar Pits also unearthed many prehistoric animals trapped in the oozing grip.

Today all of these wells are capped, and the rustic scene has completely disappeared. Wilshire Boulevard is now a six-lane, paved thoroughfare with expensive shops where once stood a beautiful grove of sycamores.

c. 1926, etching, 7" x 6"

THE FIRST PRESBYTERIAN CHURCH

The First Presbyterian Church of Hollywood was built on Gower Street in 1924, the year before a big earthquake occurred in Southern California. When the dust settled after the quake, everyone was amazed to see how firmly the building still stood. There were only a few cracks that needed to be repaired in the walls of the towers.

As this was my own church, I was particularly concerned about the freestanding finials at the top of the towers because these were located above the intersection of two very busy streets. Feeling that the towers were a possible hazard to pedestrians below, I recommended to the church board that they strengthen the structures. The board then had the finials partially removed and reinforced them with steel before putting them back into their original positions.

This church is still standing today, a place of many memories for me. It had a large Sunday School, whose buildings are not shown in this picture, but the church complex eventually occupied a good portion of the block between Franklin Avenue and Hollywood Boulevard.

1948, etching, 9" x 6½"

LOS ANGELES RIVER BRIDGE

This sturdy bridge across the Los Angeles River was used for crossing from Pasadena over to the west side of Los Angeles. Constructed of heavy timbers, its old-world appearance made it a favorite picnic area in the early years.

The Los Angeles River carried a thundering swale of water during the winter rains. In time, it became necessary to strengthen the bridge with the heavy timbers and to reinforce the bases to protect them from the debris that was swept along in the flooding stage.

The old bridge was torn down in about 1920, and later, picnicking ceased to be popular when the river's banks were converted into a concrete channel.

1930, etching, 6" x 8½"

THE OLD MISSION WINERY

The Old Mission Winery in downtown Los Angeles stood for many years as the centerpiece of the thousands of acres of vineyards which surrounded it. No doubt the men who built the winery many years ago had some of the mission architecture in mind, because it looks more like a church than a winery.

c. 1928, etching, 6" x 6½"

WORLD PREMIER

Hollywood in the 1930s was considered the world center of the motion picture industry. Nowhere was this better demonstrated than at an opening night of a first-run movie at Grauman's Chinese Theatre. The town put on its glad rags and came out to the opening to see and be seen.

I had visited several of these "openings" over the years and had seen the excitement—searchlights playing on the overhead banners and movie stars alighting from their expensive limousines to delight the crowd of spectators not content to see their favorite stars only on the screen.

c. 1928, etching, 7" x 5"

CERRITOS ADOBE

Early California settlers in Long Beach built the Cerritos Adobe with local timber and adobe blocks made, most likely, by Indians. The landmark home was near the world-famous Signal Hill oil field which overlooks the distant harbor.

The Bixby family lived in this house in former years. It was the headquarters of the Bixby Ranch, on one of the original Spanish land grants in California.

This drawing was made when the house was deteriorating, and the most alive thing in the scene was the cactus blooming in the front yard.

c. 1928, etching, 6" x 7"

SAN PEDRO HARBOR

The San Pedro Harbor, some thirty miles from the city of Los Angeles, was the principal shipping port for the West Coast; in fact, it is second only to the port in New York City. Two other major West Coast ports—San Francisco and Seattle—also handle considerable shipping from throughout the Pacific.

In this picture we see boats of various kinds docked in one of the fingers of the Los Angeles port. The tugboat in its berth on the right may have just returned from pulling a larger ship out to the ocean. The man at the center is handling cable, which was probably used in its mooring. Fishing boats and commercial steamers pass by the large warehouse across the bay.

c. 1928, charcoal, 9" x 12"

THE GRIFFITH OBSERVATORY

The Griffith Observatory, located in the hills immediately behind Hollywood, is world renowned for its spectacular contribution to the knowledge of the firmament.

Here famous astronomers use the four telescopes, each of which has a revolving and removable cover, opening the sky directly to the observer.

Founded in 1935, the observatory became an active center attracting both the professional and the amateur astronomer. There are many exhibits on the Tesla coil, weather satellites, radio astronomy, the nature of light, and other topics. Historic items, such as antique instruments, are on display to add to the study of astronomy and related sciences.

In the immediate foreground we see two of the many houses on the hills above the city and below the observatory.

1935, pen and ink, 12" x 9"

PASADENA BRIDGE (DISTANT VIEW)

A beautiful three-arched bridge spans the Arroyo Seco near Pasadena. This wide wash flows from the mountains directly behind the city. With the increase in population, this once-remote area is now full of beautiful homes.

Over the course of time this old steel-reinforced concrete bridge deteriorated to the point of being unsafe. It was patched up and left as a relic of the early days, while a newer bridge was built parallel to the old one.

n.d., etching, 6" x 8"

THE PASADENA BRIDGE (CLOSE-UP)

The old Pasadena bridge was built over the Arroyo Seco, which separates Pasadena from La Cañada/Flintridge and the City of Eagle Rock.

A small footbridge crossing the arroyo can be seen at the bottom of the picture just above the stream bed. In the background is one of Pasadena's famous hotels, the Vista Del Arroyo (View of the Arroyo).

The Pasadena Bridge has been proclaimed one of the most beautiful in America. Unfortunately, this landmark has also attracted many people who wished to commit suicide.

n.d., charcoal, 11" x 9"

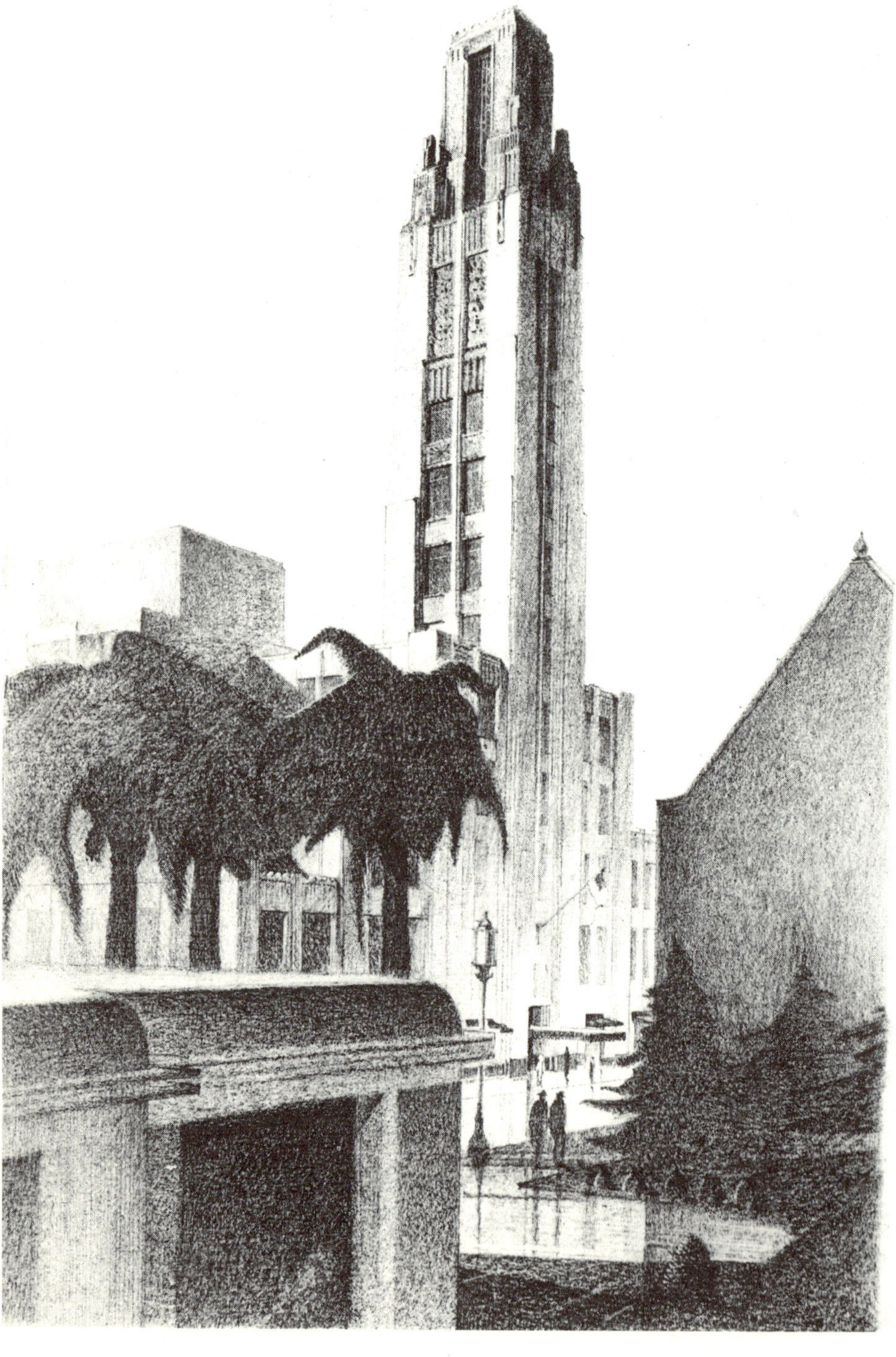

BULLOCK'S DEPARTMENT STORE

During the Depression, when there was little work for architects, I sat outside Bullock's Department Store and made a sketch of this Los Angeles landmark. As I drew, I could hear the Bullock's chimes ring out on the hour from the emerald-green terracotta tower.

Then I took the sketch inside and asked if they would hire me to do a sketch of each of their departments as advertisements for the store.

Bullock's is located on Wilshire Boulevard, which runs from the business center of the city and on through Beverly Hills to the beach at Santa Monica.

The restaurant on the second floor was a popular place for businessmen to meet their wives for lunch. During that hour there was a daily fashion show where models displayed the latest clothes, so the husbands could be warned what their wives' next purchases might be.

Bullock's hired me to draw interior sketches of each department in their store. Not only was it satisfying to see my work appear in full-page advertisements in the Los Angeles Times, but the $100 per picture was a lot of money in those days.

1925, lithograph, 13½" x 9½"

San Diego

SAN DIEGO

ANOTHER PLACE where I sketched in those early days was San Diego, where my parents used to drive our family for a vacation once or twice a year. The most important trip we made was to the 1915 Pan Pacific World's Fair, which drew international attention to the city.

By 1915 many of California's natural resources had been developed and trade had increased with the countries on the Pacific Rim. Furthermore, San Francisco was already attracting visitors that same year with its Panama-Pacific International Exposition.

These fairs were opportunities to feature the natural resources and manufactured products found on the Pacific Rim, especially California.

The two fairs were different in two important respects. First, San Diego was more Spanish, and its fair reflected the Spanish and Mexican influence not only through the blending of cultures, but also through its magnificent architecture.

Although both cities were founded by early Mexican and Spanish padres and soldiers, San Diego has retained more of a sense of the tranquility so often felt in many of the cities of Mexico.

Second, San Diego chose to house its exhibits in permanent buildings which could be used after the fair for municipal purposes. San Francisco planned to retain only one of its exposition buildings—the Palace of Fine Arts, which featured the famous Tower of Jewels and Court of the Four Seasons.

San Diego chose as its architect Bertram Goodhue, who was at the time gaining prominence as the designer of the Nebraska State Capitol, the Los Angeles Public Library, and new buildings for West Point on the Hudson River. Thus all of the buildings were of uniform style, touched by the particular genius of one man.

Today these structures, which house permanent exhibits, are located in Balboa Park along with the extensive, world-famous zoological gardens. The buildings and exhibits afford the visitor an opportunity to become more aware of California's natural resources and cultural heritage.

MAIN ENTRANCE

The most renowned of the fair's buildings supported an ornate main entrance tower located at the end of a bridge crossing a small ravine that separates the fairgrounds from a main thoroughfare. The plain plastered walls make the ornamental entrance and the tower stand out by contrast.

Here Bertram Goodhue demonstrated his skill as a designer by combining the neo-classical Mexican style of architecture with his own, which was akin to early Romanesque. In the Southern California setting of green eucalyptus trees and bright sunlit skies, his red tiles and white-washed buildings were a delight to behold.

1935, pen and ink, 14″ x 10½″

HORTICULTURAL BUILDING

This view shows the horticulture building, whose red-tiled roof and white walls blend harmoniously with the eucalyptus trees and the large pool dotted with waterlilies.

This building housed an awesome exhibit of exotic plants, many from tropical areas of Central and South America. On the trees and shrubs displayed were also many nesting birds.

1935, pen and ink, 10½" x 14"

FIESTA DANCERS

During the Fair, lights attached to poles reflected in the pools and made a fairyland of each courtyard. Every evening, an outdoor dance orchestra combined its music with sounds of water from the main fountain.

On moonlit nights, dancers moved among the shadows of the tall trees. Sailors forgot the rigors of the ship as they escorted girls through this park-like setting.

The carefree pleasure of dining and dancing under the stars was accented by the clicking of castanets and an occasional shout from a twirling performer in full Spanish costume.

1935, pen and ink, 12" x 8"

STATUETTE

Tucked away under the trees and other vegetation were little statues of California's heroes, such as Father Serra, Portola, and Crespi. In this picture we see a statuette of the Greek god Pan, adding a playful touch to the scene.

1935, pen and ink, 14" x 10½"

FAIR BUILDINGS

Buildings of the fair in general were of a light, almost whimsical style—Mediterranean to be sure, but with the distinct touch of the architect's fantasy. A pleasant place for mothers to push their strollers. They also sometimes brought the family dog who lazed about in the shade or lapped cool water from the pools.

Birds in abundance from nearby San Diego Bay perched in branches of the trees and added their cheerful songs to the tranquil setting.

1935, pen and ink, 14" x 10½"

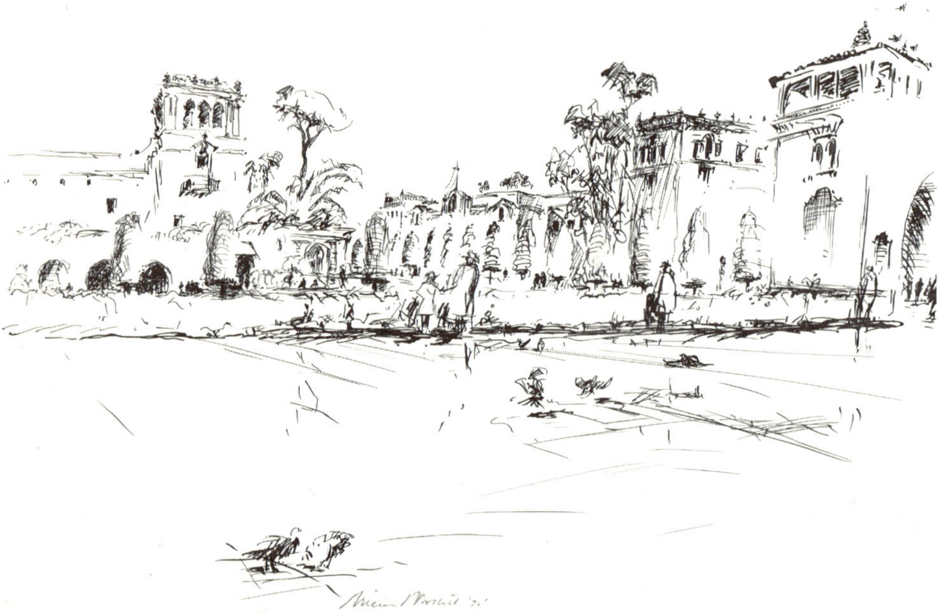

COURT OF THE SEASONS

Buildings were placed sufficiently far apart so there was ample room for plantings and broad walks. Some buildings were joined together with delightful loggias.

The tall eucalypti with their extended swaying branches brought a fresh scent on the breezes off the bay. The beauty of that uncrowded, uncluttered setting convinced me that San Diego had doffed its hat to the visitors and said, "Enjoy our Fair. Thank you for coming."

1935, pen and ink, 10½" x 14"

CALIFORNIA MISSIONS

CALIFORNIA MISSIONS

I ORIGINALLY BECAME interested in the California missions through Mrs. Forbes. Her historical library as well as her own writings about the early days intrigued me.

She and her brother were bellmakers by trade, and she is the one who pressured the California Highway Commission to erect the series of mission bells marking the route of what the early Spaniards called the King's Highway. Out of my conversations with her came the idea of including sketches of some of the missions in my portfolio of important California places.

Back in the eighteenth century, King Carlos II of Spain learned that the Russians were establishing settlements down the northern coast of what is now the Pacific Northwest. To protect Spain's interests in Mexico, Carlos sent a military expedition (1769) to establish a chain of presidios and secure the unexplored coast of what we now call southern California.

The Franciscans, led by Father Junipero Serra, accompanied the soldiers in order to convert the Indians and set up missions alongside each of the outposts. By 1823 the padres had founded a chain of twenty-one missions extending northward from San Diego to Sonoma, spaced about a day's journey (forty miles) apart along the road known as The King's Highway.

Most of my drawings of the missions were made in the 1930s when money was scarce. My parents often drove me to some of the missions and waited patiently while I sketched.

A hundred years had passed since the missions were secularized (1833) and the buildings began to suffer the ravages of weather and vandalism. The churches were used for shops, barns, and storage; the bricks and tiles were taken for building materials in other structures. Earthquakes and rains further damaged them, until they fell into ruins.

Gradually these historic places began attracting artists and photographers who extolled the picturesque beauty of the landmarks. Toward the end of the nineteenth century their importance became more and more evident to citizen's groups who undertook restoration projects.

By the time I made my sketches, much work had already been done. Today all the missions have been either rebuilt, restored, or at least stabilized to prevent further erosion.

SAN GABRIEL ARCANGEL

This mission was originally founded in 1771 and moved four years later to its present site, where a permanent church was begun in 1791.

In the construction of mission buildings, the padres usually copied the architecture of Mexican and Spanish churches. The San Gabriel Arcangel Mission, however, is unlike the others because the padre there patterned the mission after the Moorish Cathedral of Cordova, Spain, where he was born and raised.

The missions were all built of adobe blocks made from the large deposits common to the area. The adobe was reinforced with rough straw and formed into blocks of about 4″ x 12″ x 18″. During the curing in the sun the blocks often became warped, accounting for the uneven spacing of the joints, where a mixture of lime, sand, and asphaltum was used as mortar.

Not having glass, the windows in general were small and closed with wooden shutters. The mission walls were one to two feet thick, without reinforcement, so that they depended on their thickness for strength. The padres relied on Indian labor for building the missions and decorating the interiors.

San Gabriel was completed six years later (1797), only to be damaged in the 1812 earthquake. Not until 1828 was it repaired.

I chose this view because it showed clearly the Moorish capped buttresses and the long narrow windows. Such elements of design appealed to me and unconsciously shaped my own architectural style, training my hand and eye.

c. 1932, etching, 4″ x 6″

The church at San Juan Capistrano was the seventh mission, founded in 1776, the same year as the signing of the Declaration of Independence.

Construction of the church began in 1796, and it took nearly ten years to complete what was a thriving mission complex. This building lasted only six years until the earthquake of 1812 destroyed it. It was never rebuilt during the mission period, and its tiles and timbers were carried off.

The mission was being restored when I first saw it, so this sketch was drawn from a picture someone had made when the building was in ruins.

1935, charcoal, 11" x 14½"

SAN JUAN CAPISTRANO

Restoration of these mission buildings had been attempted in the 1860s and again in the 1890s but none of these was as complete as the work in the 1920s by Father St. John O'Sullivan. He tried to reconstruct what he concluded was original stone work, the Mexican designs, and the lovely gardens.

Common Spanish and Mexican influences included a central courtyard; the motifs at the doors, windows, and the altars; Roman arches in the arcades that run the length of the buildings; the use of the red tile for roofing; the high timbered ceilings, made mostly from pine trees that were burned and scraped down with stones; and adobe blocks made of local material.

When I went there to sketch, the town of San Juan Capistrano had not been built up, but was just a place by the side of the road. Because the restoration was underway, the whole mission grounds were surrounded by a board fence, so I had trouble finding a suitable vantage point from which to sketch.

1965, charcoal, 10" x 15"

SANTA BARBARA

Founded in 1786, Santa Barbara's church, built eight years later, was destroyed by the 1812 earthquake. The present church, with only one tower, was begun in 1815 and completed five years later, a second being added in 1831.

Another earthquake caused damage in 1925, and donations came in from all over the state to restore this "Queen of the Missions."

The Santa Barbara Mission sits on a hill overlooking the city and the Pacific Ocean. It is the only mission which has had continuous service since its founding.

Although the view I chose to sketch doesn't show the Roman facade, the towers are plainly visible from my position to the west of the walled cemetery.

The banana man and his dog were there, but later I added the farmer with haystack, standing where once was the mission orchards and the majordomo's quarters.

n.d., charcoal, 13" x 14"

SAN FERNANDO REY DE ESPAÑA

Founded in 1797, this mission was the seventeenth in the chain. The original building, completed in 1799, was replaced in 1800 and again in 1806. That church fell in the 1812 earthquake and underwent several restorations in the 19th and 20th centuries until it was destroyed beyond repair in the earthquake of 1971. An exact replica of it was completed in 1974.

To sketch the mission, I drove from Los Angeles north thirty miles to San Fernando in my old open-top Buick roadster. The church had fallen into ruins, and the only major building left standing was the long adobe mission house with its nineteen arches.

In particular, I wanted to sketch the ceiling of this colonnade, which had been burned to make it look old. The picture shows the adobe blocks underneath the cracking plaster.

I put the padre in later from memory. He had come out to the entrance of the arcade to see what I was doing, but I did not want to ask him to remain while I took time to sketch him.

1940, etching, 9" x 7½"

SAN FERNANDO REY DE ESPAÑA

The chapel had not yet been restored when I was there. Since the roof was missing, the exposed beams were open to the sky. I liked the way the light came in through the window, so I placed a couple kneeling at prayer in the shaft of light.

1940, etching, 7" x 6"

SAN FERNANDO REY DE ESPAÑA

The sparkling fountain in front of the San Fernando Mission is shaded by beautiful weeping willow trees, where many birds flit about entertaining the tourist. The arcade in the background is one of the loveliest in the mission chain.

1940, etching, 8" x 6"

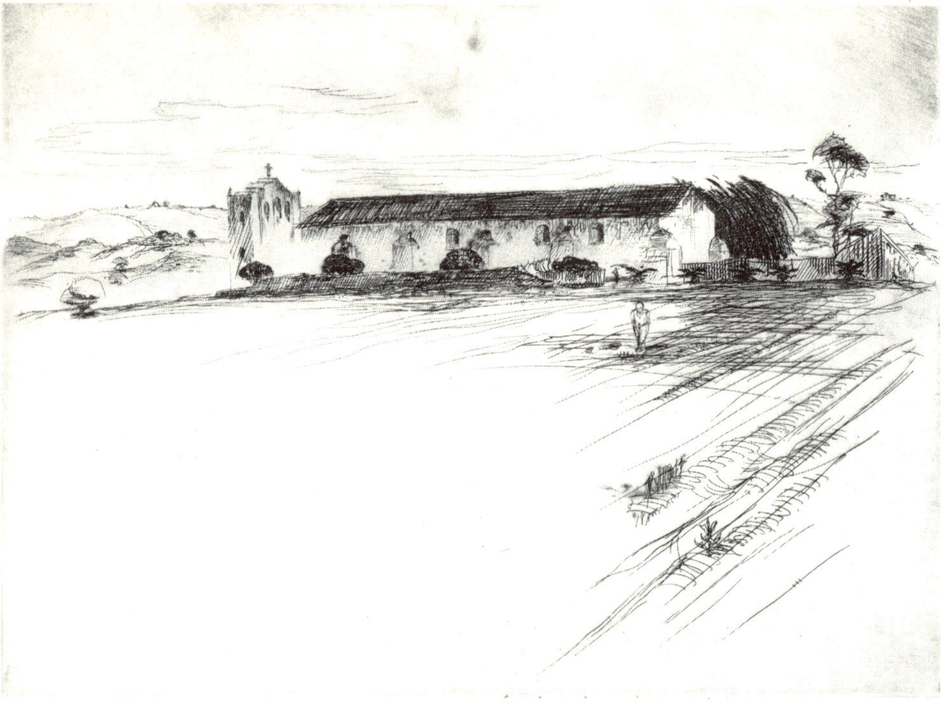

SANTA ÍNES

One of the last to be founded, this mission prospered because of its early reliance on help from the other more established ones.

Founded in 1805, the mission grew rapidly in the fertile valley that surrounded it, and soon a building program was underway to provide a church and other necessary structures. The whole quadrangle was completed shortly before the 1812 earthquake which destroyed or damaged the entire complex. A new church was dedicated in 1817 and remains to this day.

After the secularization was enforced in 1834, the mission was used as a family home and a blacksmith shop for a time.

A twenty-year restoration project, begun in 1904, had been completed by the time I visited the mission. One afternoon my parents drove me here from Pasadena to make a sketch. It was a race to beat the sun because I had to draw fast enough to finish before dark.

I chose this vantage point to make use of the long shadows of the late afternoon. When I came to make the etching from the sketch, I added the man digging in the field.

1925, etching, 8" x 11"

Catalina Island

CATALINA ISLAND

CATALINA ISLAND has long been Southern California's playground. Its name conjures romance and mystery because of its link with honeymooners and pirates' buried treasure.

As a child I was fascinated not so much by "buried treasure" as by the fact that people could live on an island completely surrounded by water and connected to the rest of the world only by boat.

My interest in Catalina was further piqued because the island had been purchased from the U.S. Government by friends of our family, Captain and Mrs. Hancock Banning. Mrs. Banning had been active in the social and cultural life of Los Angeles, where my family knew her as the president of the Assistance League.

She was involved in promoting the building of the Pilgrimage Play Theater and the Hollywood Bowl, both designed by my father, William Lee Woollett. Not only had the Bannings talked about Catalina, but many of my friends had vacationed there and brought back enchanting pictures of the island.

In 1919 the Bannings sold the property to William Wrigley, Jr., the chewing gum magnate who formed the Catalina Island Company for its development.

At the time, the natural inhabitants were wild goats, sheep and pigs which grazed on the grasses of the rugged, mountainous terrain. The long and narrow island has an area of about 75 square miles and is partly covered with trees, mostly eucalyptus.

Wrigley developed the island with lovely homes, including his own mansion overlooking Avalon Bay. His company built the luxurious hotel, Saint Catherine's, on the gently sloping shores of Avalon Bay on the southeast coast. Later he added The Casino, a large dance pavillion.

I never had the opportunity to visit Catalina until after I was married. In 1929, while trying to eke out a living from my drawings, I found a way to take my young family to Catalina. I asked the Catalina Island Company to give us a week's vacation at Saint Catherine's in exchange for a series of sketches they could exhibit as advertisement for the island. This was my first experience at bartering.

WRIGLEY MANSION

As a boat enters the harbor, the Wrigley Mansion is on the left side of the terraced hill above Avalon. The mansion looks across Avalon Bay and the Pacific Ocean to the distant shores of Santa Monica and Long Beach, on the mainland.

From the veranda of this stately old mansion, Wrigley had a spectacular mountaintop view of the surrounding hills, the ocean, and the village on his very own island.

c. 1929, pen and ink, 18" x 12½"

HARBOR VIEW

Passenger boats tied up across the harbor are dwarfed by the much larger pavilion on the right. To the left is the center of the town, with its stores, apartments, and smaller hotels facing the waterfront.

As we walked along the main street curving around the bay we could stop and eat at any of the small concesssion stands or buy souvenirs at the curio shops. Further ahead we passed the St. Catherine's Hotel, a short distance from the pavilion.

This was in the early days, when Catalina was a mecca for young people vacationing from the mainland, mostly with their families. The city set up a small tent village on the beach to accomodate the tourists.

Catalina was also the permanent home for many people who had retired from the business world and the social whirl of San Francisco, Los Angeles, and other major cities across the country.

c. 1929, pen and ink, 12½" x 18"

CENTRAL SQUARE

The Spanish fountain in front of the Esplanade was chiefly decorative, as there were no horse-drawn vehicles. The island's largest fountain, it occupied the middle of the main street near the piers, boathouse, and ornamental boxed palms. The dance pavilion, visible in the background, was only a short walk away.

The highly ornamented fountain was covered with genuine Mexican tile, whose gay colors and patterns blended with the festive dress of the island visitors.

Nearby, many sunbathers enjoyed the fine stretch of beach while snacking on food they brought over by boat or purchased on the island.

Another pleasant activity was riding in the glass-bottomed boat and seeing close-up the schools of tropical fish which abounded in the clear waters of the lagoon.

c. 1929, charcoal, 12½" x 18"

AVALON HARBOR VIEW

This general view of Avalon Harbor shows the Wrigley Mansion high on the hill to the right. At the base of the cliff lies the bath house across from the ferry and pleasure boats anchored at the two piers.

The small town of Avalon extends to the right up the canyon where most of the people live who run the hotel and maintain the town. I sketched many scenes from this hillside spot overlooking the city, where I could see the small houses with their red-tiled roofs and open porches. Below them, commercial buildings reach down to the water's edge, where a passenger boat is tied up at the pier.

One day as I was sketching an enchanting island scene I noticed a small boy who watched me for a long time before coming closer and asking, "Mister, don't you ever use an eraser?"

c. 1929, pen and ink, 13½" x 18½"

BOATS IN THE HARBOR

This sketch looks toward Avalon past many fishing boats and a passenger boat tied up to the pier. Many people came to Catalina to fish in its waters, with barracuda being the favorite and the most plentiful catch in these tropical seas.

Another pier for fishing extends back to the main street paralleling the bay. Smaller fish considered the shallow bay a haven from predators in the deeper ocean waters on the west side of the island.

The bay was a happy playground on the lee side, protected from direct ocean winds. Many pleasure boats lay at anchor there year round, and in the early days before air travel, regular passenger boats plied the waters between Santa Monica and the island.

c. 1929, pencil and charcoal, 19" x 12½"

ST. CATHERINE'S HOTEL

St. Catherine's Hotel is a three-story building, which William Wrigley, Jr., had constructed to house guests who stayed for extended visits.

The hotel is set against the lovely hillsides and bordered in front by the promenade along the sandy beach. The many tall palms—one of them purported to be over one hundred years old—give verticality and sharp contrast to the low rolling hills above Avalon.

My etching of a similar view was used on the cover of the hotel's dining room menu for many years.

Many cabanas lined the beachfront and were rented for a small fee. Parents or nurses could sit in the shade and easily watch over their children, who loved to play in the warm sand and calm waters.

c. 1929, pencil, chalk and charcoal, 12½" x 18"

PAVILION

This is a view of the bathhouse on the left and the pavilion in the center background. The extended balconies of a house or two are shown facing the clear blue waters of the bay.

The permanent piers were made of logs that swayed noticeably when a large launch or ferry pushed against them.

On the right, pleasure boats bob quietly at anchor. For those people who slept in their boats at night, the nearby boathouse with its light and tower afforded a measure of security.

c. 1929, pencil and charcoal, 12½" x 18"

COVERED PROMENADE/CLOCK AND BELL TOWER

The walkway extends from the wharf and the center of town around the bay to the pavilion on the waterfront. This was covered with gaily colored canvas during the hot summer months.

Also near the center of the town, on the side of the hill, is a clock tower that chimes every quarter hour, night and day.

Many artists set up their easels in just such places around the island in order to capture on canvas both the natural and manmade beauty of the island.

c. 1929, charcoal 12" x 8½"

PAVILION

This view shows the main entrance to the dance pavilion. At the lower right of this picture, notice the series of arches over the walkway which extends from the pavilion to the harbor and on around Avalon Bay.

c. 1929, charcoal, 11" x 12"

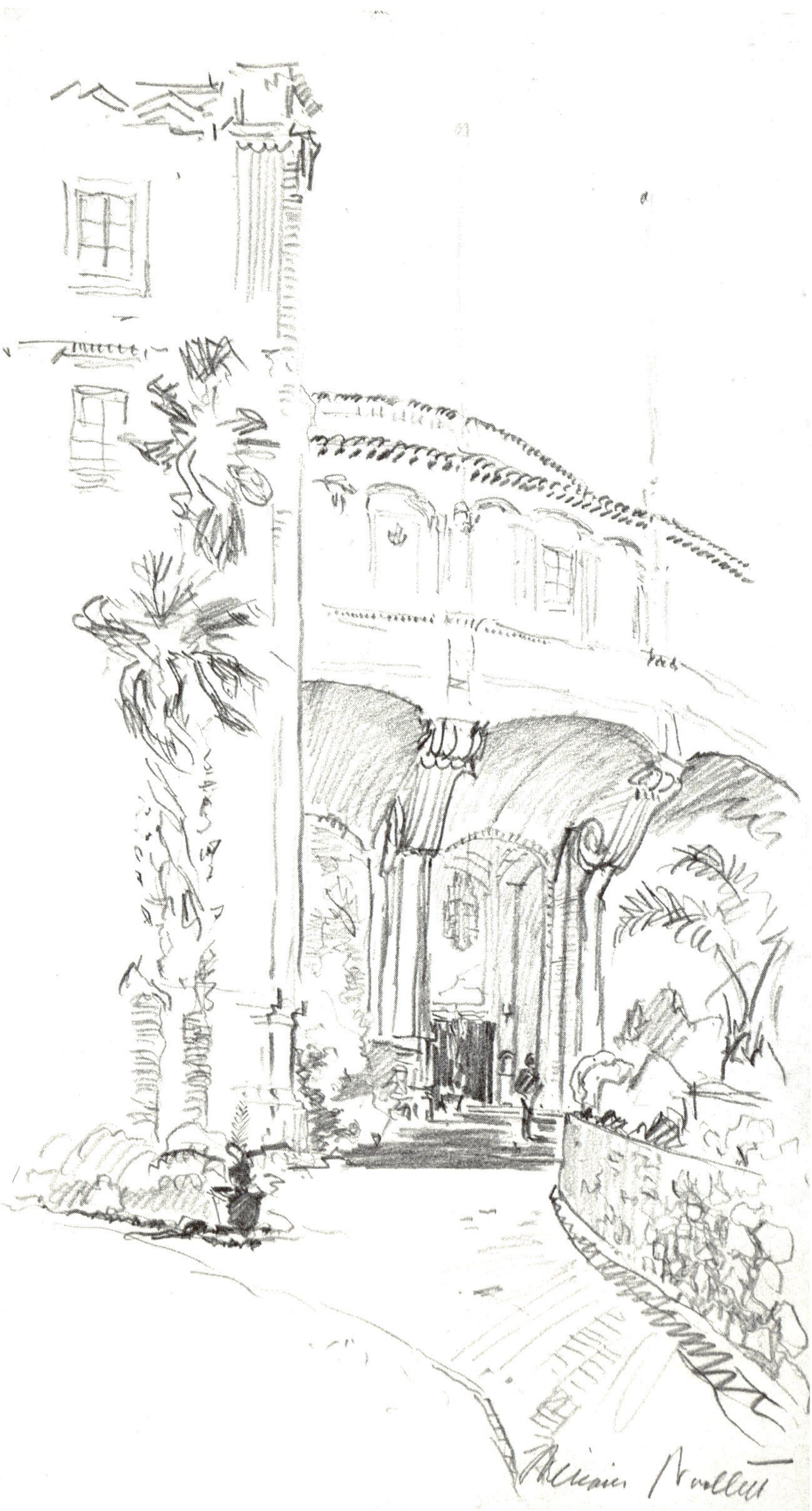

PAVILION

The ornate pavilion displays neo-Renaissance architecture designed by Sumner Spaulding. With such a voluptuous support system for the second floor, the design looks as though Spaulding was trying to be playful while still retaining a sense of order in the structure and ornamentation.

The exterior of the building has a continuous row of barrel vaults separated by scrolled brackets above pilasters. These support the overhanging second floor, thus providing more space for dancing and large parties upstairs.

c. 1929, pencil, 12½" x 7"

CLUBHOUSE

This view of the clubhouse, located on the golf course of the island, shows how the architectural style of the pavilion was carried over into other buildings on the island.

The arched walkway is supported by columns with ornate capitals.

c. 1929, pencil and charcoal, 19" x 12½"

Hoover Dam

HOOVER DAM

ANOTHER GREAT work-relief project that provided thousands of jobs during the Depression was the building of the Hoover Dam. When it was completed, it was the largest dam in the world, rising seven hundred and forty-two feet from base to crest.

Located on the border of Arizona and Nevada, the dam was built to tame the mighty Colorado River whose spring rampages had often destroyed crops throughout the Imperial Valley. Controlling these waters would also allow their diversion to meet the needs of the booming population in the southwestern United States.

As an architect I read the newspaper accounts of the project with great interest. I saw the potential not only for the public good, but also for my work as an artist.

Dam construction required the best available skills from engineers and workers alike. Many companies had made bids on the government contract which was finally won by a consortium of contractors called the "Six Companies."

The Hoover Dam was considered America's greatest engineering feat, and perhaps no other single man-made creation has benefitted America as much. The dam's mighty mass of concrete holds back the rain and snow runoff of thirteen western states. It provides a shoreline of over five hundred miles for camping and outdoor recreation. The dam's generated power travels by transmission line and its water by aqueduct over hundreds of miles to serve the greater Los Angeles area.

The drama of building the dam played continuously day and night between 1931 and 1935, and I followed the news from afar, studying the *Los Angeles Times* sketches of Mr. Owens and the pictures made by the government photographer, Mr. Glaha.

As an artist, I wanted to sketch this outstanding historic project, but I didn't have the money to travel there. Finally, when I was able to pick up rides back and forth, I was thrilled to be on the construction, to live with the workers, to witness the spectacular project, and to experience some of the dangers.

Nature also provided its own pleasant visual surprises. Often in the early morning as I approached the site from my makeshift camp at the rim of the canyon, the steel highline cables were stretched out before me. On them were myriad dew drops formed during the night, and through these the sun shone to give the effect of a sparkling necklaces, quivering eight hundred feet across the deep cleavage of the canyon.

There were tragic scenes as well—when a safety cable broke and plunged several workmen five hundred feet to their death, or in the early days when a flash flood quickly swept away workers and equipment.

As the dam progressed I increased my visits so I wouldn't miss any of the new developments and methods of construction. I was excited to be a part of it, if only as a recorder of history in the making.

Because of the immensity of this project, I have written and illustrated a separate book entitled, Hoover Dam.

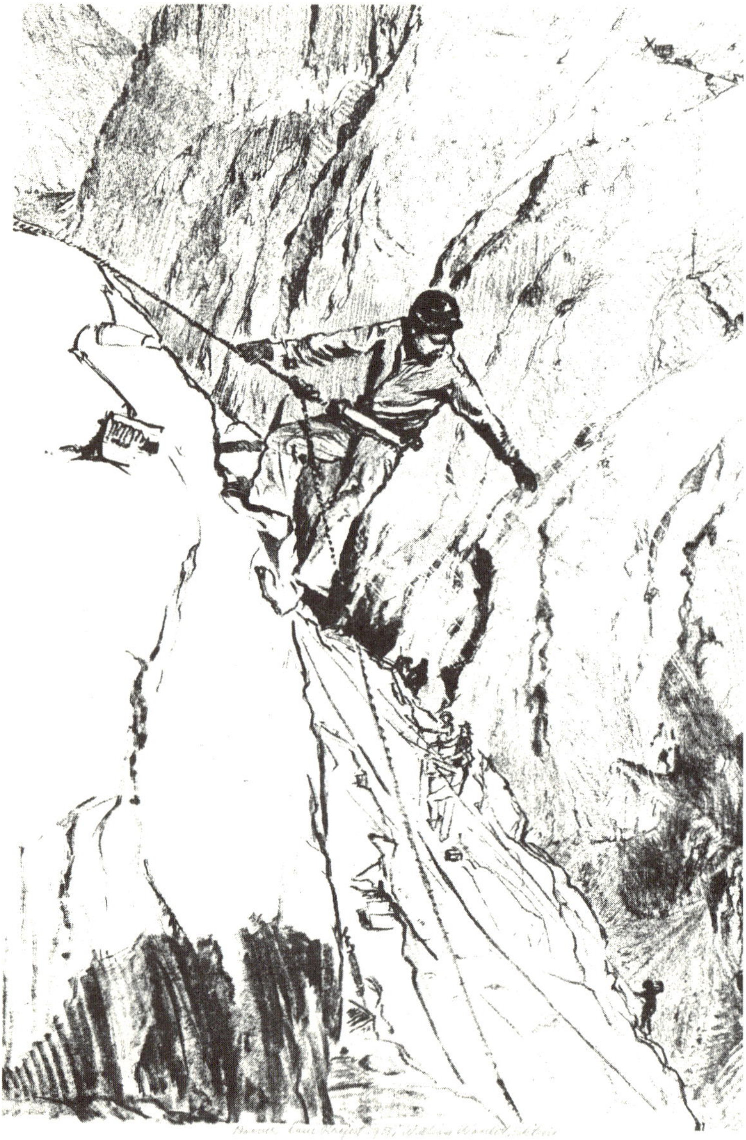

HIGH-SCALER

A high-scaler with a safety belt is hanging from a rope suspended over the side of the canyon. These trapeze artists spend their dangerous days climbing like ants up and down the canyon to clear it of debris and check the cables that support hundreds of lives every day.

Once during the sketching, I had climbed out on a steep cliff to work and then couldn't get down. Like Nathaniel Hawthorne's little boy who climbed too high, I was finally rescued with a rope let down from above.

There was also another daring, breathtaking scene I'll never forget. Two high-scalers were suspended like window washers on the surface of a cliff, working one a few feet above the other. All at once the supporting line of the scaler above broke, and he cried out as he fell. Instantly, the lower man pushed away from the cliff and grapped his helpless co-worker. Fortunately, his supporting line held under the weight of both the men, thus dramatically sparing their lives.

c. 1932-35, lithograph, 19" x 13"

NEARLY FINISHED DAM

When the dam was nearly finished and intake towers (penstock) were topping out, one could grasp a sense of the total scheme and magnitude of this construction.

The men crossing the catwalk at the bottom of the picture seem so tiny and useless, but each one's labor was necessary for the taming of the mammoth river. It took the genius of men to devise the plan whereby this could happen.

The process was gradual because each twelve-foot-square cubicle had to be cured before the one above it could be formed and poured. Each section was staggered with the rest os that each form butted up against the adjacent tower already built. Horizontal and vertical steel reinforcements were used every few feet through the dam.

After three or four curing days, the wood forms were ripped off, loaded onto eight-foot-high steel sawhorses and set afire at night. From anywhere you might be standing in the big canyon you could see the spectacle of the entire top of the dam ablaze.

A dozen men stood there with high-pressure hoses spraying the new concrete below the sawhorses to keep it from being destroyed by the heat. Thus the water flowed down the side of the dam in shining rivulets, like a mighty, scintillating waterfall.

c. 1932-35, etching, 7" x 9"

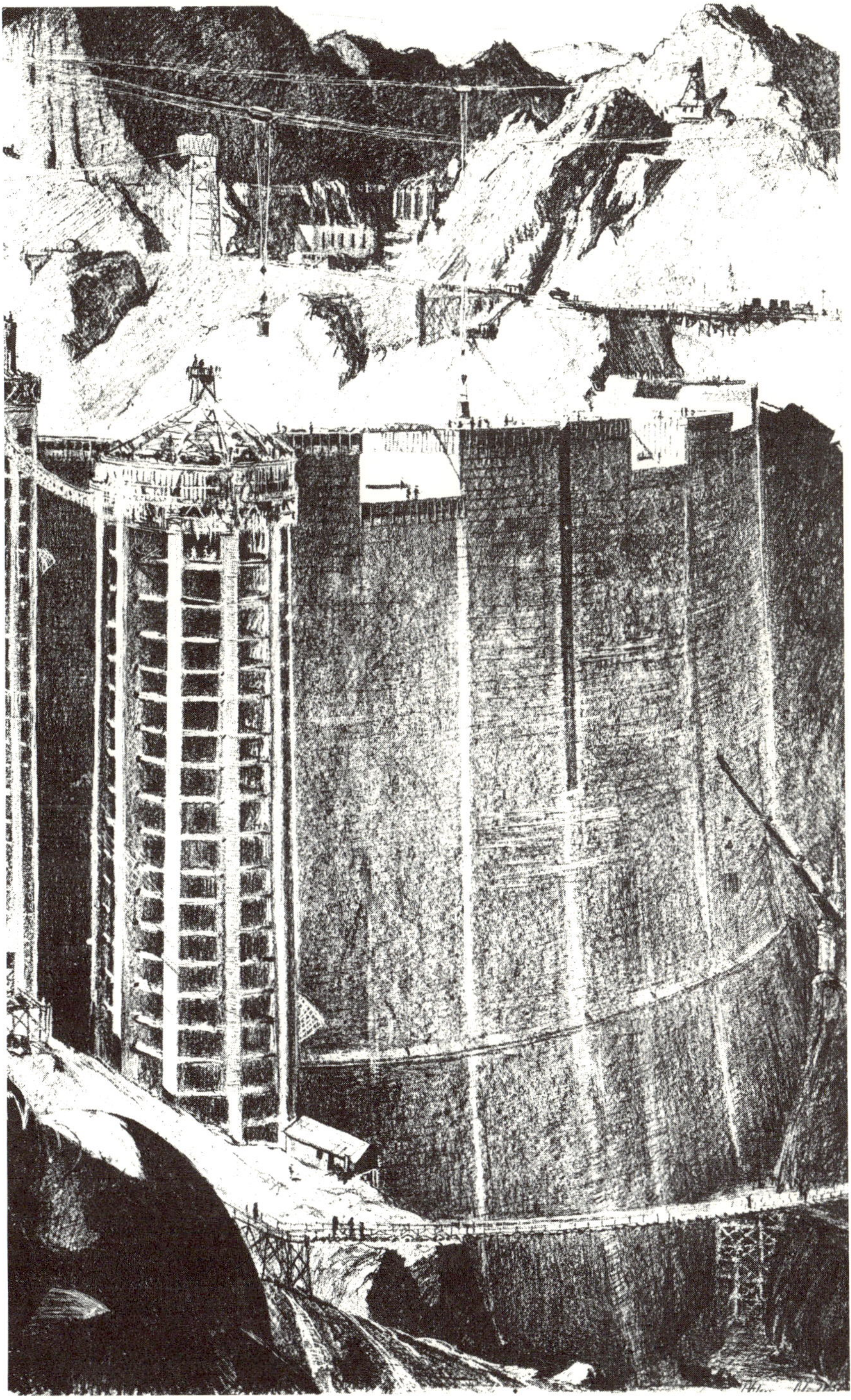

Transmission Lines

TRANSMISSION LINES

For many years Southern California suffered from a shortage of electric power, even though the Mulholland Dam did much to alleviate the problem. The City of Los Angeles recognized that its growth was hindered because it could not supply enough water and electricity for the ever-increasing demands of more homes, street lights, factories and commercial buildings.

The city fathers looked eastward to the Colorado River for a solution to their problems and built the Los Angeles Aqueduct—three hundred miles of concrete pipelines to transport an apparently inexhaustible supply of water across the desert. To bring electricity they built the Los Angeles city transmission system lines, linking the city with the new power supply of the great Hoover Dam.

These two projects, costing some $160 million, together with the Hoover Dam, completed the means by which water and power could be distributed to millions of homes, farms and factories not only in Los Angeles, but throughout the southwest.

The first problem with planning the transmission line was to decide a route by which towers and wires would cross the hundreds of miles of deserts, mountains and barren valleys.

After a feasible route was determined, then began the difficult work of clearing the land and building roads. In many places dense underbrush and huge boulders blocked the way; in others, bridges had to be built to span raging rivers. Rocky terrain required blasting foundation holes with dynamite.

In addition to all the expected construction problems, field mice began eating coverings on the ground wires which then had to be buried about a foot below the surface.

Concrete bases deep in the earth supported the tower legs which themselves extended several feet below ground level. The steel towers rested on four legs which measured three feet across at the base.

Construction crews lived in nearby base camps and worked rain or shine. As soon as one tower was completed, the crew would move on to the next site. Then another crew would arrive at the first to string the power cables and install the ground lines as lightning rods to carry static electricity from the towers and defuse it into the ground.

Because of my interest in Hoover Dam, I naturally became involved in recording the engineering projects which developed from it. I obtained permission from the Bureau of Power and Light in Los Angeles to follow the men as they worked over mountains and through deserts.

I drove out from Los Angeles to visit the camps around Barstow, spending a day or two at a time in the desert. I carried a board to sketch on and drew the men in their various stages of work. I didn't draw as many sketches of the Transmission Line because I had to fit this project in around my other work as an architect.

SURVEYING

The surveying crew searched through low hills and hot deserts for sites where the power towers could be erected. The condition of the ground was very important because the footings for the legs had to have a firm foundation. Often these were dug or blasted out of solid rock.

Other problems hindered the work. Strong winds blew through this area, and many times underground streams had to be diverted.

All this had to be accomplished while the Hoover Dam and the adjacent power house were being constructed, so that power could be delivered as soon as possible.

c. 1935, lithograph, 16" x 11"

ROAD SCRAPER

This view shows a road being bulldozed through the low hills in order to help move supplies to the camp sites in the desert. Such roads needed only occassional maintenance by a road scraper because they were surfaced with rock and asphalt. and would never be used by the public.

After the transmission line was built, careful maintenance was needed to keep fire hazards away from the towers. Flash floods would sometimes wash out a tower leg, crippling the tower.

c. 1935, lithograph, 13½" x 19"

DESERT CREW

Here a construction crew bores holes six feet deep and three feet in diameter for the footings of the transmission line towers. The holes are dug with an auger held by a small tractor, which could easily move across the sand from tower base to tower base. Sometimes huge boulders were encountered and blasting was required to remove them.

c. 1935, lithograph, 14" x 19"

CONCRETE DOWN CHUTE

On this uneven desert terrain, men poured fresh concrete into a swiveling metal sleeve which delivered it to each footing hole so that all four tower legs would be level. A scaffolding had to be built for the wheelbarrows which carried the liquid concrete as it flowed from the mixer down the chute. On the left in front of the mixer is a truck carrying the water supply.

c. 1935, lithograph, 13½" x 18"

ON SITE

A tower erection crew assembled the steel reinforcements made of vertical and horizontal members welded together into a "form," with a central stub to extend above the ground for the attachment of the tower legs.

The reinforcement was lowered into the footing hole and surrounded with concrete, which made a solid foundation.

Then the tower leg was bolted to the steel stub protruding from the top of the form. If the tower was located on a sloping hillside or on rocks which were not level, then the stub was raised or lowered so that each leg could be firmly bolted to the adjustable form.

If no foundation could be dug through the solid rock, the tower leg would be bolted to the rock and to a precast shoe which fitted over the end of the leg.

c. 1935, lithograph, 14½" x 20"

STEEL TOWER LEGS

Workers poured concrete into the base for one of the tower legs. The concrete mixer in the background was moved from tower to tower, and a truck brought water, sand, cement, and rocks for the concrete to be mixed at each site.

Other materials were also brought by truck from a central supply house so the entire operation could be carried on in the field.

c. 1935, lithograph, 14" x 19"

EARLY MORNING LIGHT

At base camp in the early morning light, men gathered after breakfast to ride to the many construction sites in the big open lorries. Then the workers took up their various tasks, such as excavating footings, erecting the poles, or stringing the cables from pole to pole. The men carried their lunches with them, for they wouldn't return to their temporary housing until the evening meal.

The water tower in the right background was important in these desert areas, not only for human use, but also to wet the roads and keep the dust down.

c. 1935, lithograph, 11" x 19"

TOOL SHED

Workers in the tool shed sharpened tools and heated rivets in the forge on the right before placing them in steel buckets to be carried to the towers. There a "backer" would place the rivet in a hole, pushing on the round end, while the "riveter" would flatten the other end with an air hammer.

Red-hot rivets were tossed up to the workman on the tower, who caught them in a bucket and put them in place with pinchers. The rivet holes had already been punched in the steel tower members before they left the factory.

The workmen wore heavy gloves to protect themselves from the burning hot metal. They also fought blinding wind-driven sand and desert temperatures of over one hundred degrees.

c. 1935, lithograph, 12" x 18½"

HALF-BUILT TOWER

The towers were put into place piece by piece, with each separate member being bolted into place. All the towers were of the same size and construction, so the parts were made in a factory and delivered to the field for assembly. If a storm or high wind twisted or bent parts of the tower, these damaged pieces could easily be replaced.

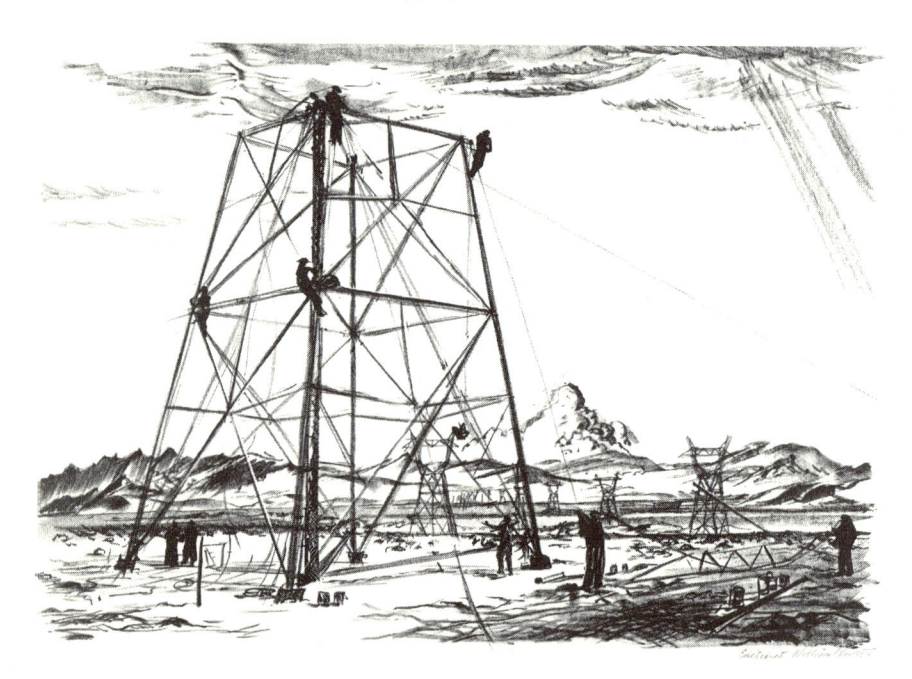

c. 1935, lithograph, 13″ x 19″

NEARLY-COMPLETED TOWER

To the left, a transmission line tower stands nearly completed. In the foreground workmen attach a steel member to a cable which will hoist it to a position above. These two towers were located in low hill country in the desert, and were designed to withstand high winds.

c. 1935, lithograph, 18" x 12½"

COMPLETED TOWERS

These towers are completed, waiting for the cable to be attached. The road in the foreground was made for delivering supplies and transporting men from the base camp to the work sites. Even after the transmission line was completed, these roads were maintained to allow service for the towers, which were buffeted by heavy winds and rainstorms.

c. 1935, lithograph, 12" x 18"

FACTORY

Transmission cable was made in this Los Angeles factory. The picture shows spools of copper strands being threaded into an assembler which twisted the strands and pressured them together to produce a single cable. The cable emerged red hot and when cooled was wound onto a larger spool to await delivery to the construction area. There it was either strung as an aerial wire or buried as a ground wire.

c. 1935, lithograph, 13½" x 18"

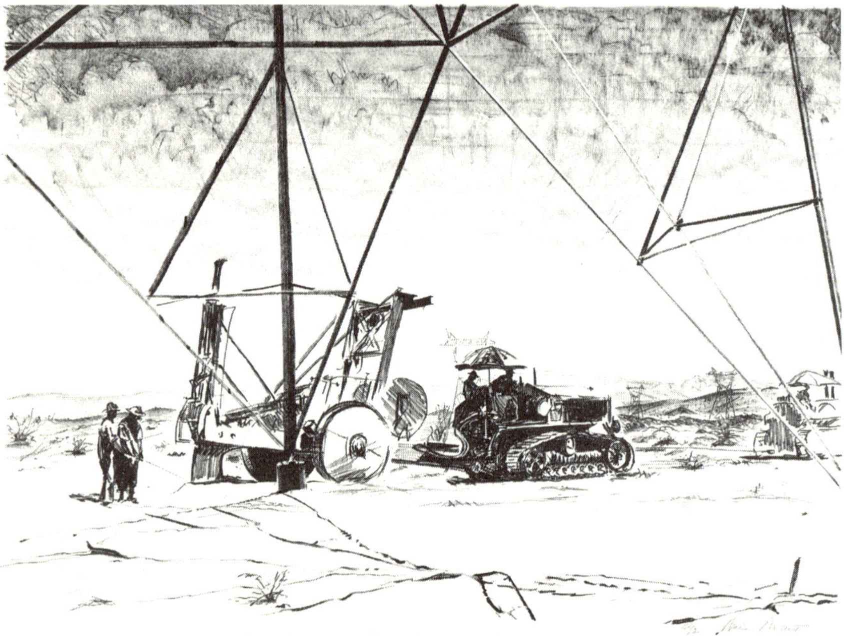

TRACTOR AND GROUND WIRE

The tractor pulls a cart on which is mounted the cable for the ground wire. The blade on the cart dug a foot-deep trench in which the line was buried under the desert floor. Each tower was grounded so that, during electrical storms, the high-voltage charge would not destroy the tower, but be carried down into the ground instead.

c. 1935, lithograph, 13½" x 18"

AQUEDUCT

LOS ANGELES AQUEDUCT

EXCEPT FOR A strip of land along the California coast, the southwestern part of the United States is arid and inhospitable. Although the Colorado River watered large portions of this area, it flowed capriciously, alternating between floods and drought. Settlers pushing west from the central and eastern states could not depend on it to sustain life.

As the population swelled, there was a pressing need for more reliable sources of water. By the early 1920s, engineers found a way: taming the mighty Colorado River and distributing its waters more consistently for a steady source of water.

Once the Hoover Dam was completed, along with the Parker Dam further downstream, the next step was to construct an aqueduct to carry the water from the Colorado River to the greater Los Angeles area.

Under the leadership of William Mulholland, civil engineer extraordinaire, some four hundred miles of concrete pipeline were laid through a series of low mountains and burning deserts.

DESERT VIEW

Here we see a view of the aqueduct as it sweeps through one of the smaller desert areas between the diminishing fingers of the California Coastal Range.

After the trench for the aqueduct was dug, large concrete pipes ten feet long were lowered into place and then cemented together. The trench was then refilled and marked by a series of iron stakes to indicate its exact location.

c. 1935, lithograph, 18" x 12½"

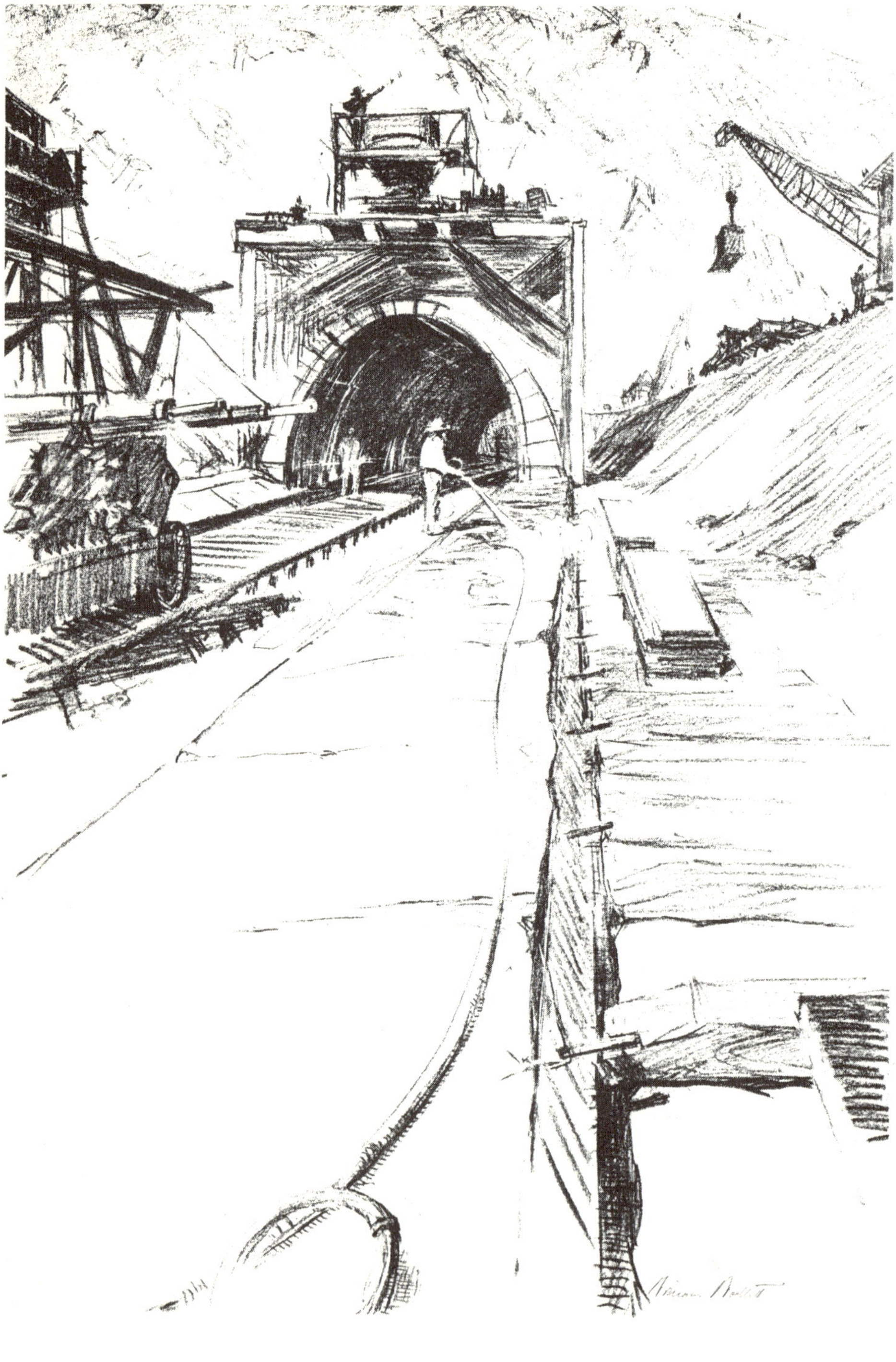

TUNNEL ENTRANCE

This view of the Los Angeles Aqueduct shows a tunnel through one of the small fingers of the coastal range. A concrete tunnel lining had to be poured to protect the pipe from cave-ins.

A cement mixer followed the construction on a parallel desert road above the trench, on the level of the desert floor. A crane swung buckets of concrete from the mixer into the hopper, which then transferred the cement to a rolling jig running along a track. The jig delivered the mix to the tunnel whence it flowed by gravity into the forms.

c. 1935, lithograph, 19" x 13"

All-American Canal

THE ALL-AMERICAN CANAL

DURING THE TIME I was drawing at the Hoover Dam, I had been following the progress of the All-American Canal through newspaper articles and photographs. It was only a matter of time before I got there to make some sketches.

Formed of concrete, the canal carries water from the Colorado River after it drops through the powerhouses at Hoover Dam. The canal outlet is from the Parker Dam, which was under construction a few miles below Hoover Dam.

The All-American Canal, like a venturesome snake, winds its way through mountain foothills, deserts, and fertile fields of the Imperial and Coachella Valleys to deliver precious water to farmers of the region.

Many times, while visiting construction camps along the Canal, I watched men excavating the great ditch or blasting through the mountains. On these visits I lived with the superintendent at the construction camps and ate with the crew.

Many of the men lived in small towns along the way, although those with wives and children remained in Los Angeles or at small campsites around Boulder City. As the Canal progressed the crew moved forward with it.

Each time I drove out from Los Angeles to meet the job, I inquired along the way where the crew was. As soon as I got to the work site I would begin sketching the activity, whether it was building roads, cutting brush, blasting a tunnel or building a small bridge over a dry desert riverbed.

DIGGING

This view of the canal shows the trench being formed with the use of huge dragline buckets and an immense crane whose arm can reach over into the canal to scoop up the sand and swing it out to the side. Here we see three cranes doing similar work.

Tons of sand had to be removed before workers could install the canal's concrete lining.

The intensity of the winds in the desert was such that many times parts of this trench would be refilled with sand that had been blown in. Until the canal was actually in use, it was necessary to remove this unwanted sand.

c. 1935, lithograph, 13" x 18"

San Francisco

SAN FRANCISCO BRIDGES

I SPENT MUCH of my childhood (1906-1915) in Berkeley, and have wonderful memories of the Bay Area. I loved the feel of sea breezes coming across the bay and to watch the lights of San Francisco come on at night.

It was an exciting city for me and whenever my family wanted to visit we would board the orange trains of the Key Route at the Berkeley station on their way to The Mole in Oakland. Then we would cross the bay on the ferry with the smell of salt water and the excitement of seagulls swooping down to catch the scraps of food we tossed into the air.

The city was a bustling place. I can still remember shopping with my mother in the large stores filled with an unbelievable array of colorful, interesting things. I enjoyed watching the people with their many different ethnic backgrounds and styles of dress.

I wondered what would happen if our bouncy cable car lost its grip and rolled backwards. I relished the taste of oyster stew at the famous Cliff House, and listened to the echoes in the high-ceilinged Lurline Baths where I swam in the tanks with my two sisters.

San Francisco is still a fascinating place, and I think of it as the New York of the west. Because of this, the Bay Area population has increased greatly over the years since I lived there.

With such growth came a need for bridges. The ancient ferry boats could no longer accommodate the vast numbers of commuters who traveled daily between the peninsula and mainland communities such as Oakland and Berkeley.

I first heard about the bridges when I was making sketches of Hoover Dam. Perhaps some of the workers were hoping to get hired in San Francisco after work on the dam was completed.

Although I wanted to sketch this project, I didn't have the funds to travel to San Francisco. My friend, Mrs. Forbes, sent me to a friend, an executive of the Sante Fe railroad, who made the trip possible.

Next I knew I would need a sturdy overcoat if I was to work out on the windy bay, so I convinced the owner of a haberdashery to give me a warm overcoat in exchange for the use of my Hoover Dam etchings in his window display.

By the time I finally got to San Francisco, the Golden Gate Bridge was nearing completion, so most of my work was done at the site of the Oakland Bay Bridge.

There I persuaded the Bridge Authority to grant me a pass to ride on the workmen's trucks and boats, thus I was able to get near enough and at such interesting angles as to sketch these great structures.

To watch the construction was an impressive sight, and if I had not studied engineering myself, I would never have believed the huge steel beams could span such long distances to make those mighty bridges.

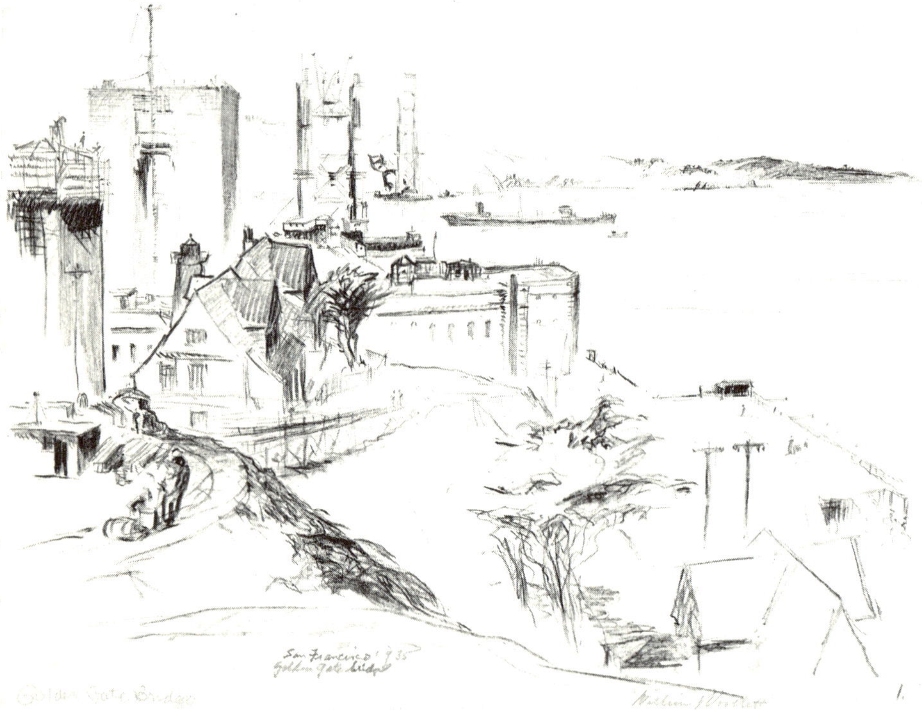
San Francisco 1935
Golden Gate Bridge
Golden Gate Bridge

GOLDEN GATE WITHOUT CABLES

In 1935, construction began on the the famous Golden Gate Bridge, largest suspension bridge in the world. It would span the treacherous ocean entrance to the San Francisco Bay and link the city with Marin County, long a rich farming, recreation, and timber area of the state.

Here, in the foreground of this picture, Fort Point lies beneath the rising towers of the Golden Gate Bridge. Nearby, an ancient house that was here before the fort was built also contrasts the old with the new.

A boat glides quietly past the construction site, belying the ever-present dangers to the men working on the bridges. From the beginning, this project was plagued with difficulties.

In order to lay foundations for the towers which support the bridges, work had to be done under water. Large hollow caissons were built 150 feet deep to the bottom of the bay. The strong currents and tides swept away many caissons and continually threaten, even to this day, those that finally were lodged into place.

Danger inside the caissons was just as great. The caissons were doubled—one inside the other—and the actual pier construction took place in the inner caisson, while the outer one protected the workmen from the intense pressure of the waters deep down in the Bay.

Each day, men would descend a rope ladder inside the inner caisson. Very slowly they proceeded, not because of fear of heights, but to avoid compression of their lungs ("the bends"). A gradual descent allowed their bodies to become accustomed to the dramatic difference in atmospheric pressure between the ground and 150 feet below sea level. This slow process of ascending and descending was so time-consuming that only a few hours of work could be completed in a day.

Only determined laborers could work so deep in the water, day after day, encased in a small steel cocoon, which they knew might become their coffin at any time. Yet, during the Depression, many men were willing to take that risk in order to have steady work.

1935, pencil and charcoal, 9" x 12"

GOLDEN GATE WITH CABLES

This view is similar to the previous drawing, but was made at a later period. At both times, I was drawing in the Presidio Park area where the first bridge tower rises out of the park promontory above Fort Point.

Here the bridge cables are being spun between the edge of the promontory and the nearly-completed towers. Lighter vertical supports will be attached to the horizontal cables and will hang down to suspend the bridge itself over the water.

Many gun emplacements are located on top of Fort Point, which was built during the Civil War to guard the Golden Gate.

c. 1935, pencil, 14" x 19½"

VIEW FROM OAKLAND

A second bridge, begun a short time after the Golden Gate Bridge, was called the Oakland Bay Bridge. When completed, it was the world's longest bridge, extending from San Francisco across the bay to Yerba Buena Island and on over to the mainland at Oakland.

The central anchorage was more massive than the piers of the Golden Gate Bridge because the Oakland Bay Bridge was four times as long and spanned the widest part of the bay.

This shows the view from Oakland looking west past Yerba Buena Island towards San Francisco. In the foreground we see the beginning of the Oakland Bay Bridge's cantilevered section as it is progressing from pier base to pier base toward the island. From there the bridge will extend across the four rising towers shown and support the cables from which the bridge proper will be hung.

In the foreground is a ferry just leaving the Oakland railway mole—the terminal for all transcontinental train service from San Francisco to the East Coast.

c. 1935, lithograph, 15" x 9½"

ROCK AND GRAVEL

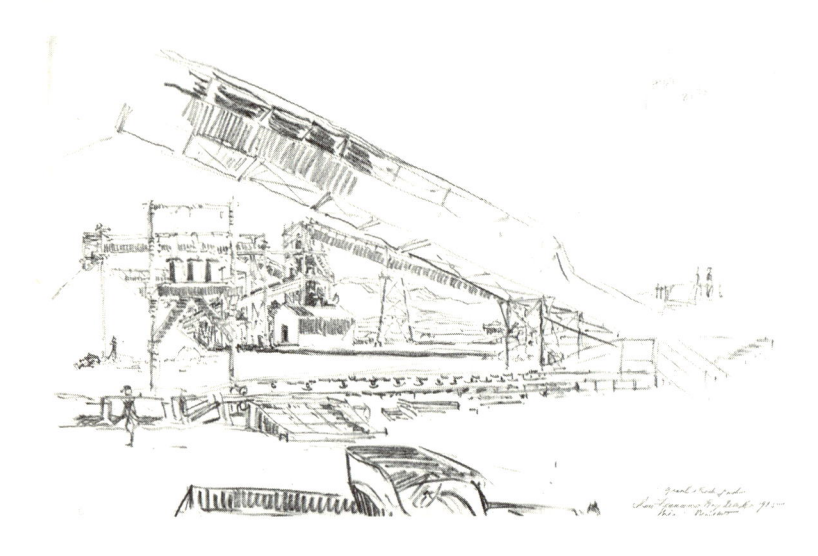

Rock and gravel were needed to build the pier foundations that support the Oakland Bay Bridge. The concrete mixer on the shore is attached to an escalator that carried the material to the San Francisco end of the bridge, where it could be carried out over the early bridge floor.

The bridge roadways themselves would be made of concrete and surfaced with non-skid topcoating.

The picture shows a ramp being built for the loading and unloading of passengers from a station platform yet to be built.

1935, charcoal, 12" x 18½"

FOUR TOWERS

These four towers will support the section of the bridge between Yerba Buena Island and San Francisco. The beginning of the center anchorage is between Towers 2 and 3.

On the San Francisco shore the famous ferry-building clock tower is adjacent to Tower 1 on the right. The waterfront buildings with their loading piers extend out to receive shipping from around the world.

The Oakland shore is in the distance to the right, with the Berkeley shore visible to the left of the tower that is near the island.

1935, charcoal, 11" x 18"

FIRST TOWER/YERBA BUENA

On the left the first tower of the Oakland Bay Bridge rises from the San Francisco waterfront. Note at the top of the tower the beginnings of the two tiers which will carry the upper and lower levels of the bridge roadway.

This sketch was made from the roof of a barge that carries materials for the bridgemakers who are working on the uncompleted tower on the left.

FIRST PIER

In the picture looking toward Yerba Buena Island, we are standing on the San Francisco shore by the first pier of the Oakland Bay Bridge. The Oakland and Berkeley shores are shown in the background with the beginnings of the cantilevered section of the bridge coming from the Oakland shore toward the island.

The picture shows the steel connectors between the two uprights of Towers 1 and 2. The lower connector will support heavy vehicular traffic, while lighter traffic and pedestrians will use the upper. This portion of the bridge will be hung from cables which will be suspended between Towers 1 and 2.

In the distance the towers look as if they are close together, but they're actually a half to three-quarters of a mile apart.

In the immediate foreground there is a hoist and two barges that transport the building materials, such as the stack of large timbers piled on the pier. On the left, the tugboat is approaching the barges to tow them out to the towers where the materials will be lifted into place by a cable pulley.

1935, charcoal, 11" x 18"

TUNNEL/YERBA BUENA

This is the San Francisco side of the tunnel on Yerba Buena Island through which the freeway bridge will pass when completed. Shown here is a view of Tower 3 under construction just before its heavy bridge cables were put in place to extend down towards this island tunnel entrance where we are standing.

1935, charcoal, 12½" x 18"

ANCHORAGE

The Bay Bridge anchorage on the San Francisco side is shown here with the two main cables well-imbedded in their concrete anchorage. The cantilevered sections will support two roadways, the one below for trains and buses, and the one above for automobiles and pedestrians.

This picture shows the structure of the bridge as it leaves the anchorage on its way over the bay toward Oakland. The cables each have a safety net attached underneath them so the workers can safely perform their jobs not only here high above the supply area but also out over the water.

c. 1936, lithograph, 9" x 16"

SECOND BRIDGE TOWER

The view from Tower 2 shows the center anchorage where the cables converge and are fastened. Alongside it in the water is a supply raft.

The worker behind the vertical compressor (in the foreground) makes sure that the hundreds of strands which make up each cable are properly in position to be tightly bound together.

Construction above the surface of the water posed such a considerable threat that most men worked with a steel safety net suspended beneath them. In places where this was not possible, the worker would tie himself to the steel pier with a belt, much as a telephone lineman works on a telephone pole.

Although the safety nets are in place under the cables, there are also handrails supported by the thick cable itself.

c. 1936, lithograph, 13" x 19½"

BRIDGE TOWERS

The concrete piers extend deep underwater to rock-bottom foundations supporting the bridge towers which will carry the first cable supports for the bridge proper. Looking from Yerba Buena Island toward San Francisco, the center anchorage can be seen on the left between two center towers.

The principal cables, being installed here, are made up of many smaller cables bound together to form a single larger one. Other smaller cables will hang down from the larger ones to hold the bridge suspended beneath.

c. 1936, lithograph, 15" x 9½"

STEEL SECTION

At the center anchorage on the right, workers are tending to the risky business of fastening a steel section of the bridge to the cable which supports it. Into the joints were hammered red hot rivets which had to be picked up with steel tongs and padded gloves.

At the bottom of the sketch, a tugboat tows the next portion of the bridge out to a spot where it will be hoisted up into place.

By the time the tugboat reaches the anchorage, the workers will be ready to receive the next bridge section and attach it to the cable above.

1936, lithograph, 14" x 19"

CANTILEVERED SECTION

The bridge supports in the left of the picture are on the east side of Yerba Buena Island. This view shows the cantilevered section of the bridge, beginning in the foreground over the shallowest part of the bay and continuing over the deepest waters and on to the San Francisco shore.

The Oakland mole for ferry boats (top right) was no longer as important after the bridge was completed, although ferry service continued between Oakland and Saucilito in Marin County.

The bridge curves around at this point, where it proceeds over the island, and from where it then continues on over to the Oakland shore.

The size of the men pictured at the bottom left of the sketch hint at the magnitude of this project.

c. 1936, lithograph, 19" x 12"

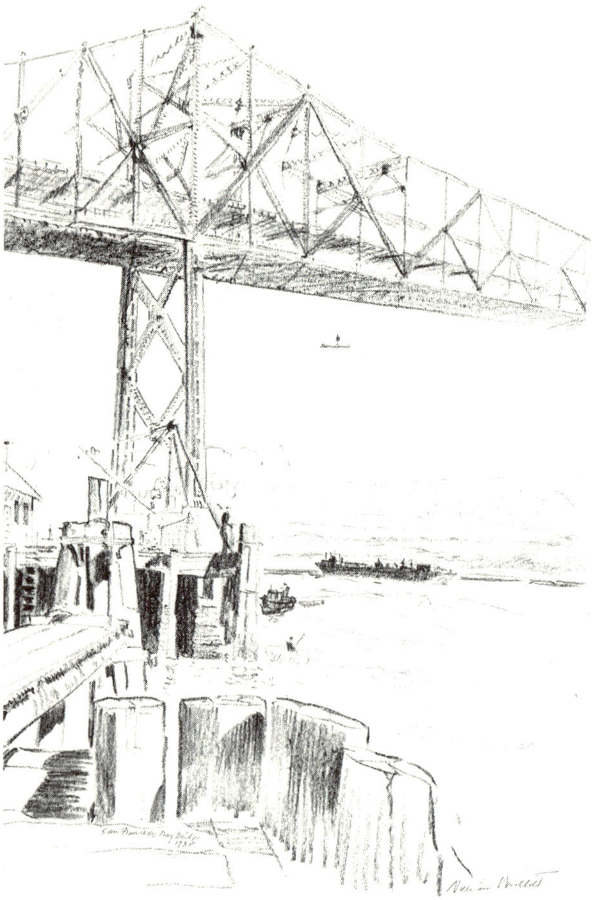

SCOW AND BRIDGE SUPPORT

This drawing shows the first support for the bridge as it leaves Yerba Buena Island for the Oakland shore. The scow in the background is bringing materials for steel members of the bridge to various locations along the waterfront. Note that the workman riding the beam is being raised from the scow below.

The Berkeley shoreline is in the background with the coastal range of mountains behind it.

Waters of the San Francisco Bay lap at the wood poles of the now-obsolete ferry slips in the foreground.

c. 1936. lithograph, 14" x 9½"

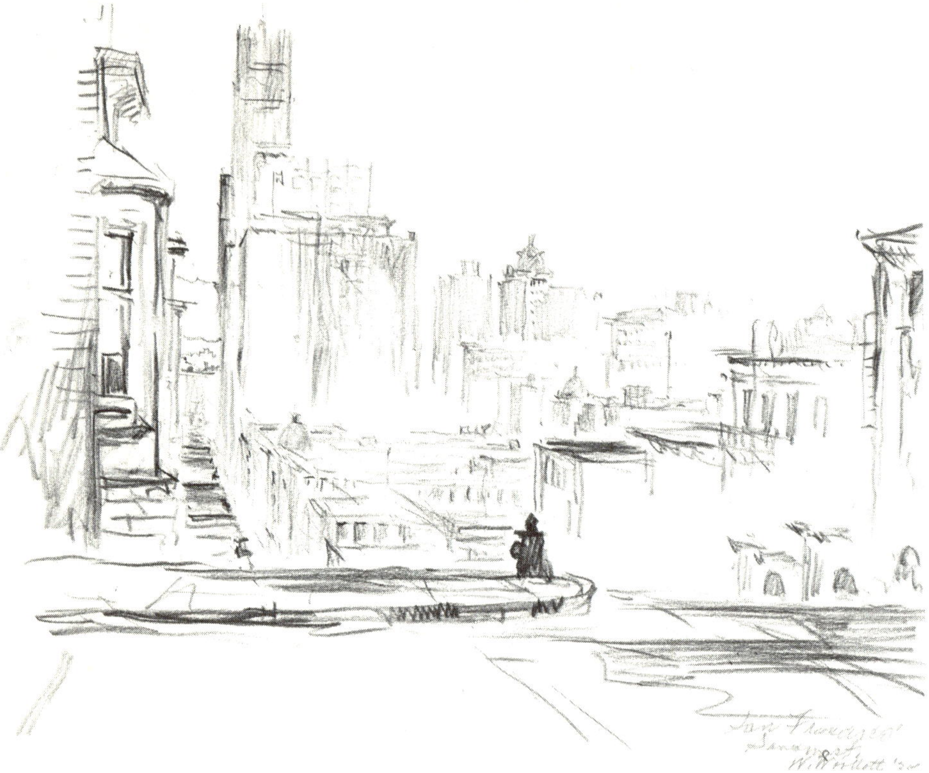

OVERVIEW SAN FRANCISCO

Some people have described San Francisco as a city of ups and downs. The terrain of the narrow peninsula on which it is built has many rolling hills covered with homes, office buildings, shopping centers and parks. In this picture we see Sansum Street running parallel to the bay on one side of the peninsula and the ocean on the other.

At the bottom of the picture, the water hydrant indicates a corner of the steep street which immediately descends to the baylevel below. We see the tops of buildings and, on the left, a small hotel's bay windows extending out over the sidewalk. This is a typical view along San Francisco's steep streets.

In the center is the city's commercial district, with a few buildings twenty to twenty-five stories high. Down the street, on the left, we have a slight glimpse of the bay and the Oakland shore in the distance.

Since San Francisco was nearly destroyed in the 1906 fire, most of the buildings that did remain exhibit the charm of their Neo-Classic and Mid-Victorian architecture, dating from the early days of the Forty-Niners. These brick and wood structures were the product of a group of architects, many of whom were trained in eastern cities or at L'École de Beaux Arts in Paris. Among the many famous names were Lewis Hobart, John Galen Howard, and Ernest Wyhe.

1935, charcoal, 19" x 12½"

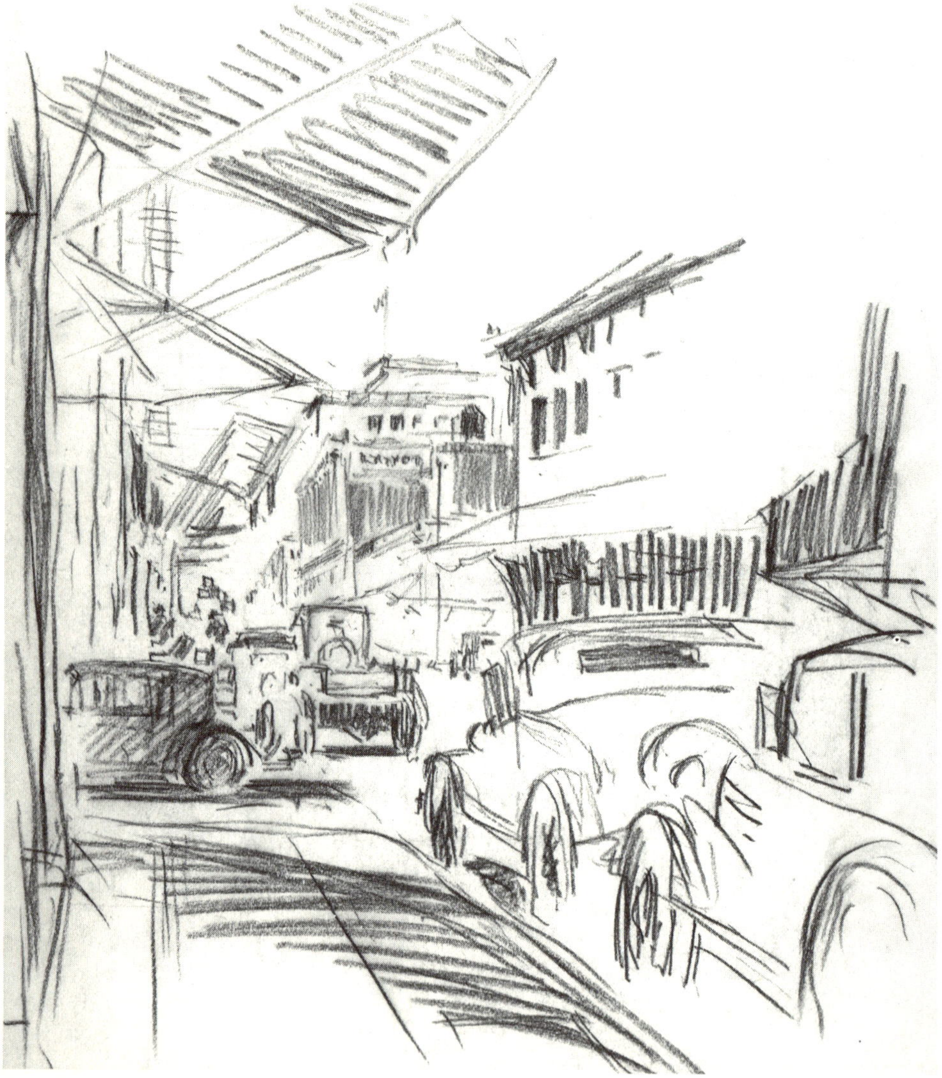

CHINATOWN

One of San Francisco's most interesting districts is Chinatown, where the visitor often feels as if he is in a foreign country. The bustle of activity goes on around the clock—with iron-rimmed wheels rolling over old cobblestone streets to a background sound of unfamiliar languages—Chinese, Italian, Portuguese and others.

This picture glimpses lower California Street, where the more modern part of the city meets Chinatown. In the background, the fashionable Fairmont Hotel waves its flag on the hill only blocks from the cacophanous din of the ethnic markets below it. The overhanging awning of the building on the left could be shading a store display window of small skinned animals for sale.

Chinatown has lost some of its earlier character. While it still exhibits the blending of the Occident and the Orient, many modern changes have occurred. Old, famous restaurants such as Sing Fat's remain, but now most of the first-floor shops cater to the tourist, and some of the well-to-do supper crowd climb winding stairs to second-story dining rooms.

When I stood on this sidewalk to draw, I could hear the sounds of many cars crowding the street, watch the awnings dancing in the breeze, and smell the rich odors from the coffee warehouse nearby.

1935, pencil and charcoal, 9" x 9½"